CW00431863

JOURNEYS INTO OXFORDSHIRE

A COLLECTION OF
INK DRAWINGS

ANTHONY MACKAY

FOREWORD BY

HIS GRACE THE DUKE OF MARLBOROUGH

First published in the United Kingdom in 1993 by
Alan Sutton Publishing Limited
Phoenix Mill · Far Thrupp · Stroud · Gloucestershire

First published in the United States of America in 1993 by
Alan Sutton Publishing Inc · 83 Washington Street · Dover · NH 03820

British Library Cataloguing in Publication Data

Mackay, Anthony
Journeys into Oxfordshire
I. Title
942.57

ISBN 0–7509–0293–0

Library of Congress Cataloging in Publication Data applied for

Typeset in 11/14 pt Bembo.
Typesetting and origination by
Alan Sutton Publishing Limited.
Printed in Great Britain by
Redwood Books, Wiltshire

Ann Boleyn's House, Henley-on-Thames

CONTENTS

Page

To the memory of
Eileen Mary Mackay (1909–57)

BECKLEY VILLAGE

FOREWORD

by

HIS GRACE THE DUKE OF MARLBOROUGH

Blenheim Palace.

Following over two years of sketching the buildings and landscapes of Oxfordshire, Anthony Mackay has produced this unique collection of ink drawings.

It is an important record of our environment, both as a visual experience and as a statement of historical development up to our time. The drawings capture on the one hand, the deeply rural character of the heart of England, and on the other, the urbanity and sophistication of Oxford itself and of the great houses of the county.

The variety and richness of building styles generated by a swiftly changing geology and guided by the influence of great artists and architects over the centuries, are affectionately portrayed.

The book is certain to encourage many others to make their own journeys of exploration, and to recognize the intrinsic qualities of this beautiful county.

Marlborough

ACKNOWLEDGEMENTS

For permission to make drawings for this volume and for giving invaluable help in compiling the historical text, I would like to thank the following:

The Hon. F.D.L. Astor of The Manor, Sutton Courtenay
The Owners of Beckley Park
Mrs Beecroft of Hanwell Castle
Mr and Mrs R.D. Bowerman of Park House, Over Worton
Mrs Willis-Bund of Combe House, Combe
Lord Camoys of Stonor Park
Mr C. Cottrell-Dormer of Rousham
Mr David Grant of The Manor House Hotel, Chadlington
Mr John Drury, Dean of Christ Church, Oxford
Castle House, Deddington
Mr and Mrs Desmond Heyward of Haseley Court
Mr J.J. Eyston of Mapledurham House
Mr and Mrs J.L. Hopkins of The Old Parsonage, Buscot
Mr Peter Jones of Gaunt House, Standlake
The Administrator of Kelmscott Manor
Mr Christopher Buxton of Kirtlington Park
Lord and Lady Macclesfield of Shirburn Castle
Their Graces the Duke and Duchess of Marlborough
The National Trust
Sir Mark and Lady Norman of Wilcote Manor
Mr and Mrs Edgar Palamountain of The Manor, Duns Tew
Mr Jeremy Parke of Studley Priory Hotel
Mr and Mrs Charles Powell of The Old Vicarage, Church Enstone
Ann Reay of The Tower, Hanwell Castle
Stephen and Anthea Savage of The Manor, Stadhampton
Lord Saye and Sele of Broughton Castle
Mr and Mrs Michael Tyce of Camilla Cottage, Waterstock
Lady Tweedsmuir of Kingston Bagpuize House
Lord and Lady Wardington of Wardington Manor
Mrs Jane Wellesley of Buckland Manor

I would especially like to thank His Grace the Duke of Marlborough for writing the Foreword to the book, and his secretary, Caroline White for her assistance. For help in processing the text, I wish to thank Professor Andrew Blowers of the Open University, and for her valuable assistance with both text and maps, I wish to thank Miss Dani Martin. Thanks are also due to Bruce and Jackie Charles of Didcot, and Claude and Alida Batchelor of Witney for occasional accommodation on my travels. Finally I would like to thank my wife Elaine, without whose support this book would not have been possible.

THE CROWN HOTEL, FARINGDON

TOM TOWER, CHRIST CHURCH, OXFORD

INTRODUCTION

The essentially rural landscape of England is reflected in all its subtlety and variety in the county of Oxfordshire. From the watery lowlands of the River Thames to the bare chalk downlands along the Berkshire border, from the steep beech-clad escarpments of the Chiltern Hills to the stone-walled uplands of the Cotswolds and the flat fenland of Otmoor, the countryside speaks of a rich pattern of gradual evolution under a predominantly agrarian society.

Oxfordshire lies at the heart of southern England, with the ancient and venerated university city of Oxford nestling at its geographical centre. Oxford is a natural focus for the region's commercial and cultural exchanges.

The underlying geology of the county determines the individual character of the regions. The rough dark ironstone of the north contrasts strongly with the pale golden limestone of the Cotswolds and with the flint and gleaming white chalk of the Downs. Clay bricks, timber and thatch are the indigenous building materials of most low-lying areas.

The once great Forest of Wychwood is now a modest remnant and although the Chilterns are generously laced with beech woods, the hunting forests of the Middle Ages have been all but extinguished.

Oxfordshire's rivers are especially beautiful, coursing down from the western uplands to join the Thames as it loops its leisurely way through the county. Widening as it goes, the Thames changes from a rustic infant to a sophisticated lady as it moves from the remote Gloucestershire border to the broad cultivated reaches between Goring and Henley.

Other than Oxford the towns are small and self-contained. Only Banbury and Abingdon show signs of independent ambitions. Smaller towns like Bicester, Wantage, Thame, Witney and Henley are still country market centres. Further down the scale, Charlbury, Burford, Chipping Norton, Faringdon and Wallingford, are little more than substantial villages. The villages of Oxfordshire make up its hidden treasurehouse. There can be few counties with such a variety of local building styles, and from the quintessentially English thatched stone cottages of Great Tew to the Cotswold masonry of Swinbrook, from the chalk structures of Ashbury to the sharply-defined timber framing of East Hagbourne and the neat Georgian brickwork of Benson, there is a condensed history lesson in vernacular architecture.

Oxfordshire has been, and still is, a prized land for settlers, conveniently situated on the western approaches to London and fairly close to both coast and midlands. Tribal settlers and invading conquerors alike have been drawn to its hospitable landscape, and there is much evidence in earth mounds and remains of buildings, that this has long been so. Prehistoric man left many tumuli and fortifications along ridges of high ground, most notably at Wayland's Smithy and on White Horse Hill at Uffington. In Roman times, military townships were built at Dorchester and Alchester, occupying key points on the Icknield Way, and villas have been excavated near North Leigh, but few important remains of this period have survived intact.

Small fragments of Saxon architecture can be seen at Langford and North Leigh churches, but again survivals are rare. The Anglo-Saxon nunnery reputedly founded by St Frideswide in the ninth century and burnt down by Danish invaders in 1002, was built over by the Normans who erected what is now Christ Church Cathedral in Oxford.

The county is rich in Norman remains, and in addition to Christ Church, which survived the Reformation relatively unscathed, we can see one of the finest parish churches of the Norman period at Iffley. Other substantial examples remain at Cassington, Cuddesdon, Bucknell and Minster Lovell. The best Norman sculpture is at Great Rollright in the tympanum over the south porch door, and in the churches of Kencot, Church Hanborough and Barford St Michael. At this time castles were built at Wallingford and Oxford, where some remnants still exist. Only forlorn earthworks survive at Deddington, Middleton Stoney and Ascott-under-Wychwood.

The abbeys of Osney, Abingdon, Eynsham and Thame all but disappeared at the time of the Dissolution and there were Augustinian priories at Bicester, Burford, Cold Norton, Wroxton and Goring, and alien priories at Cogges and Minster Lovell, but the only monastic churches to survive are at Dorchester and St Frideswide. Abbots' lodgings at Thame and outbuildings at the great Benedictine monastery of Abingdon are the only important remains.

The Middle Ages saw enormous changes in the country, and Oxfordshire was an important focus for ecclesiastical and secular building. In the late thirteenth century the first buildings of the university appeared at Merton, and the die was cast for the future of Oxford as an educational centre. Among several remarkable thirteenth-century churches, Broughton, Bloxham and Chipping Norton stand out for their beautiful window tracery, but the most impressive feature of any is the unique Tree of Jesse window in the choir of Dorchester Abbey church.

One of the earliest and finest medieval tithe barns in England stands at Great Coxwell. Built to resemble a cathedral, it is an awe-inspiring structure. Further stone tithe barns followed in the fourteenth century at Swalcliffe, Enstone and Upper Heyford, and stone bridges were constructed across the Thames at Radcot and Newbridge.

The fifteenth century introduced Perpendicular architecture to Oxfordshire with exquisite fan-vaulting in the Wilcote chapel at North Leigh, and in the panel tracery of the Milcombe chapel at Bloxham. Elegant additions to university colleges were also built during this time at All Souls, Worcester, Magdalen and St John's. The magnificent vaulted ceiling of the Oxford Divinity School was completed in 1483.

Many fifteenth-century stone houses still stand in Burford, and there are good examples of timber-framed dwellings of the period at Dorchester and Thame.

The most ancient inns in Oxfordshire are of this time. The Shaven Crown at Shipton-under-Wychwood, The George Inn at Dorchester, The Bird Cage at Thame and The White Hart at Henley are all still in use.

THE ABBEY GUEST HOUSE, ABINGDON

From 1432 to 1437 the beautiful church, almshouses and school at Ewelme were completed using Flemish craftsmen.

During the Tudor and Elizabethan period several large country houses were built, although most have been heavily modified. Substantial parts of Stonor Park, Hanwell Castle and Mapledurham have survived, and at Beckley Park on the edge of Otmoor, a moated hunting lodge in patterned brickwork stands unmolested on the site of an earlier fortified structure.

Arguably the most impressive medieval house in the county is Broughton Castle, which started life as a small fortified manor-house in 1300, and was entirely remodelled in 1554. The original vaulted rooms and the private chapel were incorporated into the Tudor house, which stands on its beautiful moated site with bridge and gatehouse.

At Stanton Harcourt, the unique fourteenth-century Great Kitchen is spectacular, and another splendid feature of the manor-house is Pope's Tower, where the poet Alexander Pope spent two years translating Homer's *Iliad*.

Grey's Court at Rotherfield Greys was originally built as a fortified manor-house in the twelfth century, and some parts of this remain around a brick-gabled Elizabethan house.

In 1605, Jacobean Chastleton House was built by a wealthy wool merchant, and has remained virtually unchanged since.

The haunting ruins of Hampton Gay Manor stand alone in the fields on the banks of the River Cherwell, a nostalgic sixteenth-century victim of a fire in 1887.

Castle House in Deddington is mainly of the sixteenth and seventeenth centuries, but still contains fragments of its medieval predecessor, and other attractive houses of this period can be seen at Kelmscott, the former home of author and textile designer William Morris, at Asthall, Finstock and Wardington.

The fifteenth-century chapel of St Michael at Rycote near Thame has some memorable seventeenth-century fittings including domed and canopied family pews.

During the seventeenth century the architect Sir Christopher Wren established the classical style at Oxford with the building of the Sheldonian Theatre. He enlisted masons from Taynton and Burford to build St Paul's Cathedral and the city churches of London following the Great Fire of 1666, and thereby made famous these craftsmen and their Oxfordshire stone. Abingdon Town Hall by Kempster, and the chapel at Cornbury Park, owe much to the influence of Wren.

Classical churches were built at Chiselhampton and Banbury in the eighteenth century, and at Nuneham Courtenay the Harcourt family built one of the grandest mansions in the county.

Rousham was built for the Dormers in 1635, but its chief glory lies in the gardens, where William Kent was employed to remodel them in 1738. He created a romantic landscape decorated with statues, follies and ruins, which sweeps majestically down to the Cherwell.

The early eighteenth century was a period of great architecture with the building of Blenheim Palace by Vanbrugh and Hawksmoor, Heythrop by Archer and Ditchley by Gibbs. Other notable smaller houses of the period include Kirtlington Park, Woodperry and Britwell Salome.

In Oxford there were many additions to the university colleges, especially to Christ Church, Queen's and All Souls. Hawksmoor also built the severely classical Clarendon Building for the University Press, and nearby, one of the city's most celebrated landmarks, the Radcliffe Camera, was completed in 1748 by Gibbs.

Substantial remodelling of Stonor Park took place in the late eighteenth century, and Pusey House was built with its charming Georgian garden chapel.

The nineteenth century started off quietly with few major public buildings of note either in Oxford or the county, but in 1843 Barry designed Eynsham Park, and in 1850 remodelled Kiddington Hall in Italianate style.

Many fine parsonages including Toot Baldon, South Leigh, Leafield and Great Milton were erected along with churches by Street at Milton-under-Wychwood and Filkins, by Scott at Leafield and Burcot, and by Pearson at Freeland.

St Peter's Church, Cassington

In Oxford, additions to the university continued apace, culminating in Keble College by Butterfield, completed in 1882. The Ashmolean and University Museums were built between 1845 and 1850.

The Industrial Revolution left few outstanding structures, but the blanket mills of Witney and the Bliss Tweed Mill at Chipping Norton are among the finest examples. Of interest also is Brunel's great brick railway bridge over the Thames at South Stoke.

The twentieth century has witnessed continued growth within the university, with the Nuffield and Wolfson Foundations, and in 1964, St Catherine's College, designed by Danish architect Arne Jacobsen, opened its doors to students, and today has settled comfortably into its landscaped environment.

The city of Oxford has expanded greatly to the east and south, absorbing the villages of Headington and Cowley. At Cowley the car manufacturer, William Morris, started building cars in 1913, and this has since developed into a massive industry supporting large numbers of people.

Despite this growth, the medieval core of Oxford with its ancient street pattern has survived. The area trapped by Thames and Cherwell at the centre remains physically intact, even though traffic pressures create some difficulties.

In the county, the towns and villages have expanded gently to cope with light industrial growth, and to house increasing numbers of commuters into London, but the overall impression remains one of predominantly rural communities whose way of life revolves around local activities.

The effect of the recently opened M40 motorway link to Birmingham has yet to be assessed, but it seems likely to transform the life-style of much of eastern Oxfordshire. The damage inflicted by such large-scale projects upon the wildlife and the countryside means the loss of hedges, woodlands and grasslands, and the habitats of many creatures. Planning policy should try to protect the natural environment from needless destruction, and aim to leave a balanced legacy for future generations.

This book records a personal choice of buildings and landscapes and is not a comprehensive guide to the county. Several places have been omitted quite randomly, and for this I offer apologies to those directly affected. I would like to believe that, by drawing certain features which seem historically and environmentally important, some impact will be made upon decisions for change and development in the future. Above all I hope that the drawings, which have given me great pleasure to make, will encourage others to go out and explore this fascinating county for themselves.

Anthony Mackay, Bedford, 1993

WARWICKS
NORTHANTS
GLOUCS
BUCKS
WILTS
BERKS
Claydon
Clattercote
Mollington
Wardington
Cropredy
Gt. Bourton
Hornton
Horley
Hanwell
Shenington
Alkerton
Balscote
Wroxton
BANBURY
Epwell
Shutford
Broughton
Sibford Gower
Sibford Ferris
Swalcliffe
Tadmarton
Bodicote
Bloxham
Adderbury
Milcombe
Milton
S. Newington
Hook Norton
Wigginton
Barford St. John
Barford St. Michael
Gt. Rollright
Lt. Rollright
Swerford
Hempton
Deddington
Souldern
Cottisford
Finmere
Mixbury
Newton Purcell
Chastleton
Salford
Over Norton
Gt. Tew
Lt. Tew
Nether Worton
Over Worton
N. Aston
Fritwell
Hardwick
Hethe
Fringford
Cornwell
Heythrop
Duns Tew
Somerton
Stoke Lyne
Chipping Norton
Sandford St. Martin
Middle Aston
Ardley
Stratton Audley
Kingham
Middle Barton
Steeple Aston
Upper Heyford
Lower Heyford
Bucknell
R. Glyme
Enstone
Steeple Barton
Churchill
Kiddington
Rousham
Middleton Stoney
Bicester
Sarsden Lodge
Chadlington
Spelsbury
Glympton
Idbury
Bruern Abbey
Ditchley Park
Tackley
Chesterton
Alchester
Fifield
Shorthampton
Wootton
Kirtlington
Milton -u- Wychwood
Ascott -u- Wychwood
Charlbury
R. Cherwell
Weston-on-the-Green
Ambrosden
Shipton -u-Wychwood
Stonesfield
Bletchingdon
Merton
L. Arncott
U. Arncott
Piddington
Finstock
R. Evenlode
Woodstock
Hampton Gay
Fencott
Leafield
Wilcote
Combe
Hampton Poyle
Charlton
Murcott
Taynton
Fulbrook
Ramsden
Bladon
Oddington
Asthall Leigh
N. Leigh
Islip
Noke
R. Windrush
Hailey
Church Hanborough
Burford
Swinbrook
Crawley
Yarnton
Wood Eaton
Horton cum Studley
Minster Lovell
Westwell
Asthall
Witney
Cassington
Water Eaton
Beckley
Holwell
Cogges
Eynsham
Woodperry
Shilton
Curbridge
S. Leigh
Wytham
Marston
Stanton St. John
Brize Norton
Ducklington
Swinford
Binsey
Headington
Forest Hill
Carterton
Cokethorpe
OXFORD
Shotover
Holton
Thame
Filkins
Kencot
Stanton Harcourt
N. Hinksey
Wheatley
Br. Poggs
Black Bourton
S. Hinksey
Cowley
R. Thame
Waterstock
Towersey
Broadwell
Brighthampton
Cumnor
Iffley
Rycote Chapel
Aston
Langford
Bampton
Northmoor
Cuddesdon
Gt. Milton
Thame Park
Clanfield
Standlake
Besselsleigh
Garsington
Gt. Haseley
Emmington
Wootton
Sandford on Thames
Sydenham
Lt. Faringdon
Newbridge
Appleton
R. Thames
Toot Baldon
Lt. Haseley
Tetsworth
Kelmscott
Longworth
Lt. Milton
Chinnor
Radcot Bridge
Hinton Waldrist
Dry Sandford
Marsh Baldon
Adwell
Crowell
Tubney
Radley
Chiselhampton
Kingston Blount
Buscot
Buckland
Kingston Bagpuize
Shippon
Nuneham Park
Stadhampton
Stoke Talmage
Aston Rowant
Newington
Littleworth
Pusey
ABINGDON
Berinsfield
Easington
Lewknor
Faringdon
Culham
Drayton St. Leonard
Chalgrove
Shirburn
Garford
Clifton Hampden
Cuxham
Hatford
Charney Basset
Drayton
Dorchester
Brightwell Baldwin
Watlington
Coleshill
Lt. Coxwell
Sutton Courtenay
Long Wittenham
Berrick Salome
Shellingford
E. Hanney
Appleford
Gt. Coxwell
Lt. Wittenham
Britwell Salome
Fernham
Goosey
Denchworth
Steventon
Milton
Benson
Christmas Common
Longcot
Brightwell -c- Sotwell
Ewelme
Watchfield
R. Ock
Baulking
Didcot
Shrivenham
Uffington
The Challows
Wantage
The Hendreds
Wallingford
Crowmarsh Gifford
Swyncombe
Stonor Park
Woolstone
Sparsholt
Harwell
The Moretons
Bourton
Ardington
The Hagbournes
Mongewell
Nuffield
Compton Beauchamp
Kingston Lisle
Childrey
The Lockinges
W. Ginge
E. Ginge
Upton
Cholsey
The Astons
N. Stoke
Nettlebed
White Horse
Wayland's Smithy
The Letcombes
Chilton
Blewbury
Ipsden
Bix
Ashbury
Idstone
Moulsford
S. Stoke
Stoke Row
Ashdown Park
Checkendon
Woodcote
Rotherfield Grey's
Henley-on-Thames
Goring
Rotherfield Peppard
Goring Heath
Kidmore End
Shiplake
Whitchurch-on-Thames
Mapledurham
Dunsden
R. Thames

GREAT TEW COTTAGES

THE IRONSTONE NORTH

Rich dark ironstone characterizes the buildings of this remote part of Oxfordshire. Snug thatched villages nestle in the folds of an undulating terrain, where steep-sided valleys swing between rounded hillocks along the Warwickshire border. In the eastern part of the region the land subsides to the glades and pastures of the River Cherwell, and the market town of Banbury stands here on what was once an important Midlands crossroads.

Early settlement is marked by the Rollright Stones, a stone circle high on the ridge between Great and Little Rollright, and by the Iron Age hill-fort at Madmarston, but Roman remains are scant.

The medieval castle earthworks at Deddington are impressive in scale, and moated Broughton Castle was begun as a fortified manor-house in 1300 and remodelled in Tudor times by the same Fiennes family which still occupies it.

Fine wall paintings in the churches of South Newington and Horley, and sculpture at Adderbury, Bloxham and Great Rollright are evidence of a strong artistic surge in the Middle Ages, and further fine work can also be seen in the tithe barn at Swalcliffe.

Great Tew is the archetypal English village, an evocative idyll of thatched stone cottages submerged under bulging hedges and teeming banks of flowers, and buried in the narrow lanes of a bygone era.

There are fine seventeenth-century manor-houses at Chastleton, Wardington and Wroxton, and many exquisite cottages and inns of this period pepper the region.

The M40 now cuts a swathe through the Cherwell valley, but impinges surprisingly little upon the landscape. The longer term effects on this peaceful backwater remain to be seen.

BANBURY

A former wool town in the Middle Ages, Banbury is the second largest in Oxfordshire, and the natural market centre for the northern part of the county. Much of the old town has been redeveloped but some fine seventeenth-century houses remain with bow windows, oriels and dormers.

The medieval church was demolished in the late eighteenth century and replaced in 1793 by St Mary's, a neo-classical design by Cockerell.

Banbury cross was built in 18[illegible]9 in the style of an Eleanor Cross. Elegant houses line the southern approach to the cross along South Bar Street and there are interesting Victorian gothic-style villas in nearby Crouch Street. In the Horsefair the Whateley Hall Hotel in impressive neo-Tudor style, and the vicarage of 1649 with gables and mullioned bays, are outstanding.

The old gaol in the market-place is early seventeenth century. Lincoln Chambers and the Unicorn Hotel are picturesque survivals from the mid-seventeenth century with half-timbered construction and overhanging upper floors.

The former Corn Exchange in Cornhill of 1857, and the Baptist chapel façade of 1839, are elegant remnants of a prosperous history.

Today Banbury has the largest livestock market in England.

ST MARY'S CHURCH, BANBURY

ALL SAINTS' LYCHGATE, GREAT BOURTON

GREAT BOURTON

Great Bourton overlooks the Cherwell valley. The small church of All Saints has an unusual lych-gate tower of 1882. The manor-house was built in the seventeenth century.

WARDINGTON

Wardington Manor was largely rebuilt in 1665 and has a fine staircase and a fireplace from this time. The splendid library was designed by Randall Wells between 1917 and 1923. The largely thirteenth-century church of St Mary Magdalen stands on raised ground at the centre of this straggling border village.

CROPREDY

Cropredy is situated in a watery landscape where the River Cherwell and the Oxford Canal run almost parallel to each other. The church of St Mary has a remarkable pre-Reformation brass lectern and several interesting monuments and, together with a terrace of thatched ironstone cottages and inns, stands against the canal. A fierce Civil War battle was fought out here in 1644.

MOLLINGTON

Mollington lies on a steep west-facing slope, with All Saints church at the high point, looking down over a tightly clustered cascade of thatched cottages. Sixteenth-century Manor Farm has a barn built in 1599.

Wardington Manor

HANWELL CASTLE AND ST PETER'S CHURCH

HANWELL

The beautiful village of Hanwell has a fascinating old church with extraordinary carved nave column capitals depicting figures with interlocking arms. In a hollow below the church lies Hanwell Castle whose stunning Tudor remains are still occupied. The Cope family built it from about 1498, but all that survives is the imposing castellated brick south-west tower, now a three storey dwelling with a spiral staircase in an octagonal corner turret. It is probably the earliest use of brick in North Oxfordshire. Attached to this tower is part of the south wing with an oriel window and later stone additions.

HORLEY

The pride of Horley is the late Norman church of St Etheldreda with its five-hundred-year-old wall painting of St Christopher fording a stream full of fish and carrying the child Jesus. Close to the church lie fourteenth-century Park House and a Georgian manor-house.

HORNTON

Famous for the golden brown ironstone quarried in this area and used widely for local buildings and for public buildings in Oxford and beyond, Hornton nestles in a sheltered valley close to the Warwickshire border. The church of St John the Baptist is of mainly twelfth- and thirteenth-century construction. The 1607 manor-house and seventeenth-century Eastgate Farm flank the village green.

ALKERTON

Alkerton clings to the side of a steep little escarpment overlooking an intimate valley and facing its neighbour Shenington, which stands on the opposite hillside. St Michael's church is Norman and has a rectory built in 1625 for Thomas Lydyat, chronologer and cosmographer to Henry, Prince of Wales.

SHENINGTON

Shenington has a beautiful hilltop green surrounded by stone houses. The Bell Inn was erected in 1700. Holy Trinity church, which has a tradition of strewing the floor with freshly cut hay between Whitsun Eve and the first Sunday after Trinity, has a few Norman remnants. Among the carved leaves of one column capital are the heads of three women and a bearded man.

EPWELL

The minute church of Epwell stands on a mound at the heart of the village. The unusually slender tower doubles as an entrance porch. Only a stone's throw from Compton Wynyates in Warwickshire, the village lies in the typically hilly countryside of this region and is overlooked by 700 feet high Epwell Hill.

SHUTFORD

The inn, church and manor-house huddle together at the centre of Shutford. Appearing to rise out of the inn, the church of St Martin has a slender perpendicular tower and rounded Norman nave columns with scalloped capitals.

The manor-house is a late sixteenth-century building with stone-mullioned and transomed windows and a four-storey projecting staircase tower on the north side. In the former Long Room, Lord Saye and Sele of Broughton is said to have secretly drilled Parliamentary soldiers before the Civil War.

BALSCOTE

Balscote has a village pond around which thatched ironstone cottages tuck themselves into the hillside. The tiny church of St Mary Magdalene has fine traceried windows and a beautiful carved oak pulpit.

Priory Farm is a fourteenth-century hall building. Grange Farm is a sixteenth-century building extended during the seventeenth and eighteenth centuries.

SHENINGTON VILLAGE

HIGH STREET HOUSES, ADDERBURY

WROXTON

Although very close to Banbury, Wroxton still retains its separate identity. Seventeenth- and eighteenth-century thatched cottages overlook the grounds of Wroxton Abbey.

All Saints church is almost entirely of the fourteenth century with the notable exception of the 1748 west tower, and stands high on a bank over Wroxton Park. The chancel and choir stalls are most probably carved by Flemish craftsmen. The reredos has fifteen finely carved panels showing Adam and Eve, scenes of the life of Christ, and the four evangelists.

Wroxton Abbey was begun in the early seventeenth century by Sir William Pope on the site of an Augustinian monastery, and subsequently passed to the North family who completed the building in the mid-nineteenth century. Lord North became Prime Minister to George III. The abbey is now a college for students of the Fairleigh Dickinson University of New Jersey, USA.

Thomas Coutts, the founder of Coutts bank, is buried at Wroxton. The village was a centre for open-cast iron mining and supplied the steel industry until bulk imports of higher grade material supplanted it.

ADDERBURY

Once a prosperous wool town, Adderbury is now a large village in two parts lying just south of Banbury. The church of St Mary is one of the glories of the county with its fourteenth-century great spire, its remarkable stone sculptures on aisle parapets and gargoyles, and its great east window. Near the church are the sixteenth-century manor-house of Adderbury East and The Grange, built in 1684. Next to this is a five-bay medieval tithe barn. Other notable buildings include a small 1854 schoolhouse, the seventeenth-century Rookery and South House of 1824.

In Adderbury West are the manor-house, a seventeenth-century remodelling of a fourteenth-century house, and Crosshill House, a three-storey, seven-bay mansion rebuilt in 1760. A side porch dated 1800 has two Tuscan columns and small Georgian stables alongside have a pedimented central block.

Both East and West Adderbury have many picturesque ironstone cottages and inns. The Red Lion, a fine old coaching inn, faces the green.

Wroxton Cottages

THE KING'S ARMS, DEDDINGTON

DEDDINGTON

In the Middle Ages Deddington was a thriving market town, but it declined in favour of Banbury after the coming of the railway. It remains a large and very attractive ironstone village with a wide market-place at the centre surrounded by fine houses and with a detached Town Hall built in 1806.

The church of St Peter and St Paul has a powerful tower with eight pinnacles and gilded vanes, built in the seventeenth century to replace the medieval tower and spire which collapsed in 1634. Next to the church stands Castle House, a sixteenth- and seventeenth-century composition of gables and towers overlooking walled gardens.

The enormous mounds of Deddington Castle lie south east of the village. Outstanding buildings include Leadenporch House in New Street, seventeenth-century Corner House, The King's Arms, a gabled inn at the north end of the market square, late Georgian Deddington House and Bury House.

SOUTH NEWINGTON

South Newington is one of the most enchanting villages of this region. The pinnacled church of St Peter ad Vincula dominates the valley; the interior reveals a display of medieval wall paintings which are among the finest in England. They depict the Virgin and Child, the Martyrdom of St Thomas tower Becket, late fifteenth-century scenes from the Passion, fragments of a fourteenth-century Last Judgement and other subjects, and are painted in oil on plaster.

BARFORD ST MICHAEL

The village of Barford St Michael clings to the side of the valley of the River Swere. The church stands high on the hill, its squat Norman tower presaging its magnificent north doorway. Built in 1150 the arch has a double order of roll moulding overset with beak-heads and separated by a band of zigzag. The beak-heads are continued down the jamb shafts. The tympanum, the infilling panel of the arch, is decorated with beaded interlace in a figure of eight. The south doorway is also Norman but less spectacular. They are among the finest Norman remains in Oxfordshire.

The George Inn is thatched and was built in 1679.

BARFORD ST JOHN

On the other side of the river, Barford St John has a small heavily restored church. Manor Farm is dated 1606 and has mullioned windows and a re-used thirteenth-century window at the rear.

Castle House, Deddington

right St Peter Ad Vincula Church, South Newington

Wall Paintings, South Newington Church

PRINTS AND IVY COTTAGE, BLOXHAM

BLOXHAM

Bloxham has a medieval street pattern made up of narrow lanes and interconnecting alleyways which create an intimate atmosphere. However, the crowning glory of the village is St Mary's, one of the grandest parish churches in Oxfordshire. Its magnificent fourteenth-century spire is prominent for miles, and there are creative stone carvings over and around the west doorway depicting a Last Judgement. The arch and jamb mouldings are filled with ballflower, leaves and birds, and the arch springing points are large carved heads. The stepped hood carries figures of the apostles with Christ at the apex enthroned between angels. Most of this stems from the fourteenth century. The Victorian east window has stained glass by William Morris, Burne-Jones and Philip Webb dated 1869, but the most elegant part of this cathedral-like interior is the fifteenth-century Milcombe chapel, a light and airy essay in Perpendicular architecture.

BROUGHTON

The romantic medieval castle of Broughton stands on its moated site only a couple of miles south west of Banbury. Built in about 1300 by John of Broughton as a fortified manor-house, it was bought by William of Wykeham, Bishop of Winchester, and founder in 1377 of New College, Oxford.

In 1450 the manor passed into the Fiennes family, or the Lords Saye and Sele, who continue to occupy it over five hundred years later. In 1554 Richard Fiennes completely remodelled the manor and built the house as we see it today. Some of the medieval rooms remain and the interior has an impressive Great Hall with decorative ceilings and a Solar wing at the east end. The fireplace in the King's Chamber has a beautiful sixteenth-century overmantel probably made by a French or Italian artist. The ceiling of the Great Parlour is a miraculous display of Elizabethan decorative plasterwork.

The castle stands against a backcloth of large trees to the east and looks out across the waters of the moat to parkland beyond. The fifteenth-century gatehouse guards a stone bridge spanning the moat.

Broughton Castle

NETTING STREET, HOOK NORTON

WIGGINTON

Wigginton stands on a hill, its slender church tower rising over the knot of low-slung cottages and farmhouses. The porch of St Giles is on an unusual squint, and inside are a stone canopied seat with carved swan and dragon finials, and two fourteenth-century effigies. A short distance from the church are considerable remains of a fifteen-room Roman villa with mid-third-century mosaics.

HOOK NORTON

Hook Norton is a large ironstone village close to the Warwickshire border in an area of beautiful hilly countryside. Celebrated now for ales brewed at the Hook Norton Brewery, it has a long history marked by the Norman church of St Peter. The font has lively carved figures including Adam and Eve, Sagittarius and other signs of the zodiac, and there are fine fourteenth-century wall paintings over the chancel arch and the south arcade.

SWERFORD

The mounds of a Norman motte-and-bailey castle lie in a field near the thirteenth-century church of St Mary at Swerford. Swerford Park is an eighteenth-century house remodelled in the 1820s and perched on the edge of a steep valley overlooking a lake and the River Swere.

SWALCLIFFE

Swalcliffe is strung out along the main road. The fine church of St Peter and St Paul has Saxon fragments, fourteenth-century wall paintings and seventeenth-century pews.

The manor-house has a thirteenth-century wing with hall and solar rebuilt by New College, Oxford between 1397 and 1423. A sixteenth-century fireplace in the hall has wall paintings over it.

The tithe barn has recently been restored. Built by William of Wykeham about 1400, it has a cruck truss roof and ten bays with buttresses.

Nearby there is an Iron Age hill-fort at Madmarston, an oval area of ramparts and ditches built between the first century BC and the first century AD.

GREAT ROLLRIGHT

Great Rollright is high in the Cotswolds. The countryside is characterized by stone-walled fields plunging into broad valleys and over long gentle ridges.

The church of St Andrew has two of the finest Norman doorways in Oxfordshire, carved with beak-heads and zigzags. The north porch has a beautiful tympanum, the stone infill over the door, decorated with stars, rings, beads and flowers. On the fourteenth-century window tracery there are sculptures of bishops, a man with an oak leaf in his mouth, a woman holding up an oak branch and a king and queen.

Between Great and Little Rollright is a 3500-year-old prehistoric stone circle about thirty metres in diameter and the third most important such monument in England after Avebury and Stonehenge. These stones are called The King's Men. Others in a nearby field are called The Whispering Knights and mark a burial chamber. On the other side of the road is the single eight-foot-high King Stone.

CHASTLETON

Situated on a high ridge of the Cotswolds on the county border, Chastleton House was built in 1605 by Walter Jones, a wealthy wool merchant, and has five gables front and back and tall battlemented staircase towers on each side. The Long Gallery runs the entire length of the top floor and has a tunnel-vaulted ceiling with rich plasterwork. The views from the gallery across the countryside are splendid. The house dwarfs the adjacent twelfth-century church of St Mary the Virgin which has a south arcade dated 1180 and a thirteenth-century font.

LITTLE ROLLRIGHT

Little Rollright is an isolated village at the end of a tree-lined lane with the tiny fifteenth-century church of St Philip standing on a small hill. The chancel has two fine tombs and a carved stone pulpit. The manor-house is a gabled seventeenth-century building. The Rectory of 1640 has three bays with mullioned windows.

CORNWELL

A picturesque village west of Chipping Norton, Cornwell lies in a valley with a running stream. The elegant Georgian manor-house overlooks formal gardens and a lake. The façade is dated 1750 but the house is much older as it was mentioned in the Domesday Book. Built around three sides of a courtyard it is a low, gabled and irregular dwelling. The stables are seventeenth century, and the dovecote has a hipped roof and lantern. The gardens were laid out by Clough Williams Ellis who is well known for his eccentric village creation at Port Meirion in Wales.

St Peter's chapel in the park has Norman doorways and a chancel arch of 1200.

NORMAN DOORWAY, GREAT ROLLRIGHT CHURCH

right CHASTLETON HOUSE

GREAT TEW

Great Tew is a beautiful village of picturesque cottages, tall trees and bulging hedges. It filters enticingly down the lanes to the brook below. Dark ironstone glows warmly under thick wedges of thatch, and in the summer gardens heave with flowers. It is one of the most evocative rural locations in England, a remarkable throwback to an earlier time.

The woodlands and park were created during the nineteenth century by a landscaper named Loudon who managed the estate between 1809 and 1811. Great Tew Park stands on a hill south of the village, although the original house has long since disappeared. The present house is a Georgian Dower House dated 1815. The stables were built in 1700.

St Michael's church is Norman with thirteenth- and fourteenth-century rebuildings leaving only the south doorway of 1170 from the original. The early nineteenth-century three-decker pulpit is in gothic style with blind tracery.

On the green are the stocks and the Victorian school, opposite which is a terrace of sixteenth- to seventeenth-century thatched cottages which includes the Falkland Arms.

THE MANOR-HOUSE, DUNS TEW

DUNS TEW

The village of Duns Tew centres upon the church of St Mary Magdalene which was largely rebuilt by Giles Gilbert Scott in 1862. Behind the church stands Duns Tew Manor, the sixteenth-century west wing of which was the original manor-house and was acquired through marriage by the Dashwood family who went on to build Kirtlington Park. The main eighteenth-century south front was built as a hunting box.

OVER WORTON

Over Worton is a charming village reached along an oak avenue. The tiny Victorian church stands on a small hillock at the foot of which are the former rectory and Georgian Worton House.

NETHER WORTON

Nether Worton has a castellated manor-house dated 1653 but remodelled in 1920. The church of St James adjoins a former schoolroom and teacher's cottage. It has Norman and Early English remnants and a wall painting depicting Christ bearing the cross.

NORTH ASTON

North Aston Hall and the church of St Mary are almost joined together on a stunning elevated site overlooking the delectable rolling countryside of the Cherwell valley. The manor-house is a fifteenth-century hall house with a Georgian cross-wing.

Cottages, Great Tew

left St James' Church and Schoolroom, Nether Worton

The Old Rectory, Over Worton

North Aston Hall and St Mary's Church

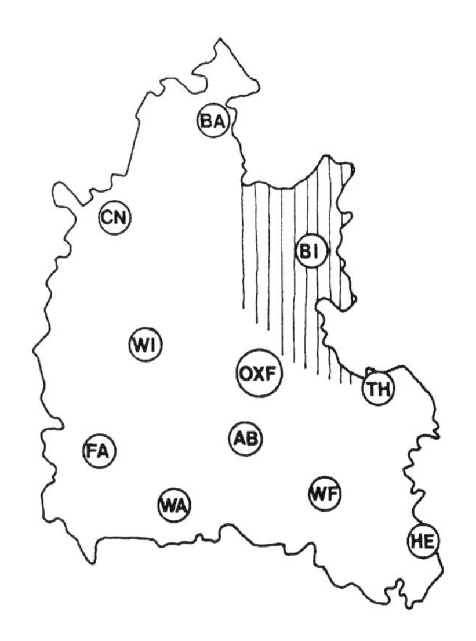

ACROSS OTMOOR FROM STUDLEY PRIORY

BICESTER AND OTMOOR

The flat farming landscape to the north of Bicester stretches from the Buckinghamshire border to the River Cherwell in the west, and is superficially rather dull. Over Upper Heyford the air is often alive with the roar of jet aircraft, and the villages seem to grit their teeth in a determination to maintain their pastoral qualities.

Further south the woods and parklands of Middleton Stoney, the magnificent faded grandeur of Kirtlington Park, and the haunting isolated ruins of Hampton Gay Manor recapture the peace and tranquillity of rural Oxfordshire.

The most remarkable part of the region is Otmoor, an ancient fen formed by the River Ray and its tributaries. This roughly circular expanse of uninhabited, marshy wilderness is famed for its unusual plants, migratory birds and in particular for its butterflies, and is a paradise for lovers of nature. Otmoor is flanked on three sides by hills which provide good vantage points for views across it.

The Seven Towns, as they are called locally, surround the moor and are in fact only villages, but each has its own distinct identity.

The pretty stone cottages of Beckley cluster on a steep slope around the fifteenth-century church, and at nearby Beckley Park, an intact Tudor hunting lodge stands on a secluded moated site.

Charlton-on-Otmoor is regarded as the capital of Otmoor and has an imposing church tower visible for miles. The former Benedictine priory at Horton-cum-Studley has been converted into an attractive hotel.

Bicester itself is the only town in this region, and as such is the focus for a lively market and shopping centre. It has a splendid twelfth-century church and several attractive town houses, but much recent expansion is featureless.

The southern edge of this region reaches to the outskirts of Oxford, and the Thame valley signals a change in building materials from limestone to timber framing and brickwork.

FINMERE

Finmere is renowned for its massive Sunday market which draws traders and buyers from a wide area. The fourteenth-century church of St Michael was restored by Street in 1856. Finmere House is a seventeenth-century rubble house refronted in brick in 1739.

MIXBURY

Earth mounds are the only remnants of twelfth-century Mixbury Castle, known as Beaumont. All Saints church has a twelfth-century nave and a Norman south doorway. The infant River Great Ouse trickles gently through the fields at the edge of the village *en route* for Bedford, the Fens and the North Sea.

COTTISFORD

Cottisford is a small village on the Northamptonshire border built around a ford over a stream, and has an interesting thirteenth-century church. The manor farmhouse with fourteenth-century remnants once belonged to the Abbey of Bec in Normandy before Henry VI gave it to his new college at Eton during the fifteenth century. Cottisford House was built in 1700 and enlarged in 1830. At nearby Juniper Hill, Flora Thompson was born in 1876. Her book *Lark Rise to Candleford* made her famous.

HETHE

The village of Hethe straggles along a winding high street and about a green at one end. Manor Farm is thatched, and the church of St Edmund and St George sits on a bank above the roadway with its curious wooden turret.

STOKE LYNE

The farms, inns and cottages of Stoke Lyne cluster loosely around the church of St Peter, which has a Norman chancel and nave, a thirteenth-century aisle, a fourteenth-century tower and a fine hammer-beam roof with animal heads holding tie rods between their teeth.

HETHE MANOR FARM

St Mary's Church, Cottisford

ARDLEY

The church of St Mary in Ardley has a massive west tower with a saddleback roof.

STRATTON AUDLEY

Only two miles north of Bicester, Stratton Audley is an attractive village with a fine fourteenth- and fifteenth-century church. St Mary and St Edburg has an embattled Perpendicular parapet and gargoyles around the porch. The manor-house has gabled dormers and backs directly onto the village street.

BUCKNELL

The church of St Peter in Bucknell is an exquisite example of Norman and thirteenth-century architecture. The old manor-house is a nineteenth-century rebuilding of a seventeenth-century house, but a plaster ceiling and a Jacobean overmantel with caryatids have survived.

BICESTER

As the largest town in this part of Oxfordshire, Bicester is an important market centre. The market-place itself retains the character of a country town with an interesting range of buildings from the sixteenth to the nineteenth centuries lined up around it.

The church of St Eadburg has Norman arches and a late Perpendicular tower of three stages with a battlemented parapet.

Bicester Priory was founded by Augustinians in the late twelfth century, but in 1537 the priory church was demolished, and the remaining buildings turned into a residence and later also demolished. The Old Priory House still stands. It is of the fifteenth century and was most likely a small guest house. The priory is a large stuccoed house opposite. The sixteenth-century Vicarage stands just to the north west of the church.

ST MARY AND ST EDBURGA CHURCH, STRATTON AUDLEY

High Street, Bicester

UPPER HEYFORD

Manor Farm barn at Upper Heyford was built for William of Wykeham of New College, Oxford. Wide stone streets lead down to the canal where views open up across to Steeple Aston on the other side of the Cherwell.

LOWER HEYFORD

An ancient stone bridge spans the River Cherwell at Lower Heyford. The village street winds downhill between beautiful ironstone houses and past the inn and the church to an old manor near the canal.

MIDDLETON STONEY

The old village of Middleton Stoney was demolished in the eighteenth century by the Earl of Jersey when he enlarged his park, leaving only the Norman church of All Saints and the adjacent motte-and-bailey castle mounds. The tree-covered mound is all that remains of Richard de Canville's twelfth-century castle.

KIRTLINGTON

In Anglo-Saxon times the Great Witan, or Assembly, was held in Kirtlington in the year 977, attended by King Edward the Martyr and St Dunstan, Archbishop of Canterbury. Stone houses are grouped around an attractive green at the heart of the village.

Kirtlington Park is a fine Palladian mansion built for Sir James Dashwood in 1742. The grand main entrance has a double staircase extending the width of seven of the nine bays.

FENCOTT AND MURCOTT

Fencott and Murcott are only hamlets but make up two of the Otmoor Seven Towns. The Nut Tree in Murcott is a charming thatched half-timbered inn beside a duck-filled pond, and there are several attractive thatched cottages along the roadside.

THE BELL INN, LOWER HEYFORD

MERTON

Merton looks across the River Ray towards Otmoor. St Swithun's church is a fine example of fourteenth-century Decorated architecture, and is one of the grandest and most ornate in this region. Jacobean choir stalls with poppyheads were brought from the chapel of Exeter College, Oxford in 1865, but replaced by unsuitable chairs in recent times.

AMBROSDEN

Ambrosden may be associated with the Romano-British general, Ambrosius Aurelianus, defeated by the Saxons in the fifth century AD. There was a sizeable Roman camp here.

The church of St Mary is mainly of the fourteenth century and the Vicarage was built in 1638, a rambling house with mullioned and transomed windows.

Castle Mound and All Saints Church, Middleton Stoney

Avenell Cottage, Kirtlington

ST MARY'S CHURCH, CHARLTON-ON-OTMOOR

CHARLTON-ON-OTMOOR

The largest of the Seven Towns is Charlton-on-Otmoor with its dominant fourteenth-century church tower peering over the fens. Inside St Mary's there is a remarkable rood screen and loft made in the early sixteenth century and sumptuously carved, painted and gilded, with linenfold panelling below and richly carved uprights. There are several fine stone thatched cottages along the broad main street.

HORTON-CUM-STUDLEY

Horton-cum-Studley stands on a hill to the east of Otmoor, and looks across toward Charlton. Studley Priory is on the site of a Benedictine priory founded in 1176, and the house was built by John Croke in 1539 with a long gabled range, and a projecting north wing with a bell-turret converted into a chapel in 1639. The two-storey porch is of the seventeenth century, and the shields of arms over the entrance are dated 1587 and 1622. The stables were built in 1666 but the remaining additions to the house were during the nineteenth century. It is now a hotel.

Almshouses in the village date from 1639, and the church was designed by William Butterfield and built in multicoloured brick.

BECKLEY

Beckley is a pretty stone village clinging to the side of a prominent hill on the southern rim of Otmoor. The mainly fifteenth-century church of St Mary has particularly beautiful stained glass and several wall paintings.

Beckley Park is an unspoilt Tudor hunting lodge standing in a woodland on an ancient moated site. In the ninth century it belonged to King Alfred and after the Conquest passed to Robert D'Oilly. In 1540 the castle was acquired by Lord Williams of Thame, who built the present house between outer and middle moats. Well-preserved, it is built of plum-coloured brick with black diapering and has stone mullioned windows under square hoods. At the rear three gabled towers cluster at the centre of the façade. The house is private and not open to the public.

NOKE

The lonely little village of Noke lies at the end of a cul-de-sac lane at the southern edge of Otmoor, and has a tiny thirteenth-century church built by Gundrada, William the Conqueror's daughter.

Studley Priory, Horton-cum-Studley

Beckley Park

HAMPTON GAY

Hampton Gay is a lonely village with only three houses including seventeenth-century Manor Farm. A footpath crosses the water-meadows to the tiny church of St Giles, and passes the gaunt and neglected ruins of the manor-house, a late sixteenth-century house abandoned after a disastrous fire in 1887. The Cherwell flows serenely through this beautiful landscape and across the river the elegant spire of Kidlington church rises out of the fields.

HAMPTON POYLE

The church of St Mary in Hampton Poyle has some fine stained glass and a fourteenth-century chancel arch. Poyle Court is a seventeenth-century house refronted in 1800 with battlemented parapet and Tudor-style windows.

ISLIP

Edward the Confessor was born in Islip in 1004. The River Ray meets the River Cherwell here, and there is a delightful stone bridge over the Ray near the Swan Inn. The village is built up a hillside, stone cottages lining the lanes and culminating at the top in the church of St Nicholas. The church was granted to Westminster Abbey by Edward in 1065, and the north arcade dates from 1200. The chancel was rebuilt in 1680 and the church was restored in 1861. The large stone Rectory was erected in 1689 and the schoolhouse in 1710.

STANTON ST JOHN

Much of Stanton St John is owned by New College, Oxford, which has its arms on the village sign. St John's church stands on a mound at the centre of the village, and has a splendid Early English chancel dated 1300, with some beautiful medieval stained glass. The early sixteenth-century bench ends in the chancel have unusual double poppyheads with human or grotesque animal heads back to back. The seventeenth-century house of John White stands opposite. He founded the Massachusetts Company, which sent settlers to start the new colony in America.

ST GILES' CHURCH, BLETCHINGDON

BLETCHINGDON

Stone cottages and the Black Head Inn surround the spacious tree-lined green at the centre of Bletchingdon. The village stands on a ridge overlooking Otmoor to the east and the Oxford canal to the west.

St Giles's church is a sturdy thirteenth-century building on the edge of Bletchingdon Park, the grounds of a Palladian villa by James Lewis, who remodelled the early eighteenth-century house in 1782 for the Earl of Angelsey. The magnificent stables are built around a courtyard.

Ruined Manor-House, Hampton Gay

Church Cottages, Islip

THE GLYME, THE EVENLODE, THE WINDRUSH AND THE COTSWOLDS

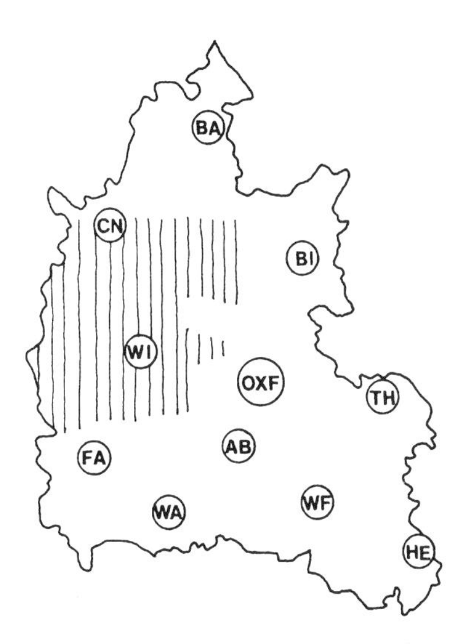

COMBE VILLAGE

This western arc of Oxfordshire stretches from the banks of the River Cherwell to the Thames in the south and contains a rich seam of delightful countryside, many great houses and countless picturesque stone villages. It is divided by the waters of the Glyme, Evenlode and Windrush as they search for the Thames, and the region reaches up into the fringes of the Cotswolds.

Remnants of the once great Forest of Wychwood lie at the heart of the region and there are further extensive woodlands around Ditchley Park and Eynsham, but much of the area is open farmland.

To the west the fields are enclosed by drystone walls, and the presence of sheep is a reminder of the once great woollen industry which helped to build and sustain the elegant towns of Chipping Norton, Burford and Witney during the late Middle Ages. To the east the land shelves steeply to the River Cherwell, enfolding the Astons and caressing the splendid gardens of Rousham Park.

The Glyme winds and twists its way from the high ground outside Chipping Norton, through the attractive stone village of Enstone to pass through Kiddington Park and Glympton Park where it is dammed to create lakes, before moving on to greater things at Blenheim. The Evenlode sweeps from stone-walled Cotswold fields to pass through Charlbury, and then loops back and forth under the railway before finally meeting the Thames to the west of Oxford.

The Windrush flows through some of the finest countryside in the county. Burford with its spectacular high street lined with elegant houses and inns, and Witney, famous for blanket making since the Middle Ages, are built almost entirely of pale Cotswold limestone, and command the western highway from Cheltenham to Oxford.

The architecture of the region is at its best in the churches of the woollen towns and villages, in the splendid mansions at Ditchley, Cornbury, Heythrop and Rousham, and in the manor-houses of Stanton Harcourt, Shipton-under-Wychwood and Kelmscott. There are also countless smaller treasures including the Fettiplace monuments at Swinbrook church, the ruins of Minster Lovell Hall, and the villages of Asthall, Bampton and Broadwell.

MIDDLE AND STEEPLE ASTON

The villages of Middle and Steeple Aston are perched high above the Cherwell valley and built in pale Cotswold stone. St Peter's church at Steeple Aston is large and was built between the thirteenth and fifteenth centuries. The monument to Sir Francis and Lady Page is a splendid Baroque work dated 1741 and sculpted by Scheemakers the Elder. The churchyard is overhung by a magnificent great sycamore tree.

The old school of 1640 had a bellcote added in 1877. Radcliffe's Almshouses were founded in 1660 by Brasenose College and rebuilt in 1814. The Grange is a Georgian house transformed into an ornamental castle in 1830. Butler's Cottage is a cottage orn of 1830. Other interesting buildings include Manor Farmhouse, Grange Cottage and Orchard Lea.

ROUSHAM

Rousham village lies outside the grounds of Rousham Park. Rousham House by Sir Robert Dormer dates from 1635 and stands on a ridge over the River Cherwell. During the eighteenth century the gardens were landscaped by William Kent with groves, cascades, statues from Italy and walkways. The seventeenth-century stone dovecote has dormer windows, a lantern and a revolving ladder-swing access to the nests. Kent also remodelled the house.

St James's church has a magnificent 1581 monument to Sir John Dormer and his family.

TACKLEY

Tackley nestles in the Cherwell valley, the spacious green flanked by thatched houses and Manor Farm with its medieval dovecote. A Tudor gateway dated 1615 is the only remnant of the manor-house. St Nicholas church lies apart on a low hill, and has a fine lych-gate, a beautiful south arcade and good monuments.

SOUTH FRONT, ROUSHAM PARK

Dovecote, Rousham Park

BRANDON FARMHOUSE, SANDFORD ST MARTIN

SANDFORD ST MARTIN

Sandford St Martin church has an Early English chancel of 1273. At the centre of the village is a medieval cross base and shaft, and nearby stands Brandon Farmhouse with its sixteenth-century front, and Sandford Park with its landscaped gardens, lakes and eighteenth-century stone bridge.

STEEPLE BARTON

Steeple Barton sits in a hollow by the River Dorn. The church stands apart. Barton Abbey has seventeenth-century stables with a wooden Tudor bell-turret staircase.

HEYTHROP

Heythrop is dominated by the magnificent Baroque mansion of Heythrop House, built in local stone in 1706 for the first Duke of Shrewsbury by Thomas Archer, and set in parkland with extensive woodlands. It was restored in Italian style by Waterhouse following a fire.

The estate village has a Victorian church, and the older disused church of St Nicholas stands separately in a field. Only the fourteenth-century chancel remains, with a Norman doorway reset from the vanished nave.

Jane Dormer, a close friend of Mary Tudor, was born at Heythrop in 1538, married a Spanish duke and left England during Elizabeth's reign.

KIDDINGTON

Kiddington House stands next to St Nicholas church which was rebuilt in 1845 by Scott. Kiddington Hall was remodelled by Barry in 1850 in Italianate style with a five-bay façade.

GLYMPTON

The village of Glympton nestles in a wooded vale by the River Glyme. Glympton Park is a mid-eighteenth-century house adapted in 1846, and stands in an elegant parkland setting enhanced by lakes formed by damming the river. St Mary's church is Norman and was restored by Street in 1872.

left NORTH STREET SCHOOL, STEEPLE ASTON

KIDDINGTON HALL

right ST MARY'S CHURCH, GLYMPTON

CHIPPING NORTON

Chipping Norton is in the north-west corner of the region and is very much a Cotswold market town whose wealth was based upon wool from the fifteenth century onwards. The wide sloping market-place is flanked by several imposing buildings including the 1842 Town Hall, a neo-classical design with a pedimented Tuscan portico.

The church of St Mary is one of Oxfordshire's finest. The fourteenth- and fifteenth-century interior is dominated by the elegant nave structure with its full height piers supporting the timber roof, and the almost continuous band of glass at clerestory level which floods the church with light.

Up the hill from the church are some stone almshouses dated 1640, with eight gables and tall chimney stacks.

On the western outskirts of the town, the chimney-stack of the former Bliss Tweed Mill rises from its domed base on a four square and solid looking building. Built in 1872 to the design of George Woodhouse of Lancashire, it is a powerful expression of Victorian industrial architecture.

INTERIOR OF ST MARY'S CHURCH, CHIPPING NORTON

ENSTONE

The village of Enstone is divided by the deep valley of the River Glyme into Neat Enstone and Church Enstone.

The Great Hoar Stone is nine feet high and marks a burial chamber. Church Enstone fringes Heythrop Park and looks across to its fine avenues of trees.

The church of St Kenelm has a Saxon foundation, but the earliest work in the south aisle is of 1180. The south aisle and chancel are of the thirteenth century, but major extensions and modifications took place in 1450. The Norman south porch doorway has zigzag patterning. The 1633 tomb of Stevens Wisdom has the effigy kneeling before his own tombstone.

Near the church is a barn built by the Abbot of Wynchcombe in 1382. It has six bays and is 72 feet long and 26 feet wide. The roof is of cruck construction. The Old Vicarage by C.R. Cockerell stands in delightful walled gardens alongside the church.

Church Lane, Chipping Norton

St Kenelm's Church and the Former Rectory, Enstone

left The Crown at Enstone

KINGHAM

Kingham is a farming village south west of Chipping Norton near the Gloucestershire border. The spacious green is at one end, and the village street leads between mellowed stone houses to the fourteenth-century church of St Andrew. The Victorian carved stone pew ends are unusual, and there is an interesting monument to a colonel in the 52nd Foot regiment who played a significant part under Wellington at Waterloo.

CHURCHILL

The church tower of Churchill is an exact copy of Magdalen tower in Oxford, but about two thirds the size. The interior of the church is Georgian. Warren Hastings was born here in 1731, rising to become Governor-General of India.

An uncut stone on the green is a memorial to William Smith, the eminent geologist, who produced the first geological map of England using fossils to ascertain the age of rock strata.

Lime Tree Cottage was built in 1694.

BRUERN ABBEY

Bruern Abbey was founded by Cistercian monks in 1137 but no traces of the buildings remain. The present house was built in 1720 for the Cope family in local Baroque style with a seven-bay front. The Oxfordshire Way passes along the eastern side of the park.

CHADLINGTON

Chadlington stretches for about a mile along a slope in the Evenlode valley. Stone cottages and inns line the road and the seventeenth-century manor-house stands next to the church of St Nicholas in a commanding position, with broad views across to Wychwood Forest. The eight-foot-high Hawkstone crowns a nearby ridge. Sir Henry Rawlinson, who deciphered inscriptions on the Rock of Behistun from the empire of Assyria, was born and raised here.

CHADLINGTON MANOR

SPELSBURY COTTAGE

SPELSBURY

The charming village of Spelsbury sits in the valley of the Evenlode. The Norman church of All Saints was rebuilt in the eighteenth century by the Earls of Litchfield, and has an interesting monument to Sir Henry Lee and his wife of 1631 with kneeling children and doll-like infants.

CHARLBURY

Charlbury is a delightful country town in the Evenlode valley. Church Street leads downhill to the church and is a well-contained space lined by pretty houses and The Bell Inn with its two-storey bay windows flanking the entrance. St Mary's church has an arcade of Norman arches and columns and some fine fourteenth-century window tracery. The Friends Meeting House in Market Street was built in 1779. A small museum in Market Street gives a flavour of nineteenth-century life in Charlbury.

SHORTHAMPTON

The tiny village of Shorthampton is an isolated and peaceful place, enjoying long breathtaking views back across the Evenlode to the stone-walled landscape beyond. The endearing little church of All Saints has Norman, thirteenth- and fourteenth-century elements, and some fine fragmentary wall paintings, a stone floor and some box pews.

COMBE

Combe stands on a steep hill above the Evenlode, which curls about below it. The unspoilt church of St Lawrence was rebuilt on the hilltop by monks of Eynsham Abbey, to replace the Norman church which sat down on the river bank.
Combe House is the former rectory and is a part-Tudor two-storey house with mullioned windows and square hoods with stepped gables at each end.

The village green has a homely inn, and winding lanes lead away from it. The sawmill in the valley next to the railway has a working steam-powered, nineteenth-century beam engine.

STONESFIELD

Stonesfield was a mining village, the source of the stone roofing slates used in the northern part of the county, and on many Oxford colleges. The area is pitted with mines and shafts, but the last mine closed before the First World War.

DITCHLEY

Ditchley House by James Gibbs was built for the 2nd Earl of Litchfield in 1722. It stands on high ground to the east of Charlbury, in a wooded landscape and park designed by Capability Brown in 1770. William Kent decorated the interior.

THE BELL HOTEL, CHARLBURY

COMBE HOUSE, COMBE

ASCOTT-UNDER-WYCHWOOD

Ascott-under-Wychwood lies snugly in the Evenlode valley. Grey stone houses surround the church of Holy Trinity, which was mainly built in 1200, with later windows and a fifteenth-century upper tower.

Manor Farm is a sixteenth- and seventeenth-century gabled house, with a barn of the same date and a brick and half-timbered granary supported on staddle-stones. The castle of Ascott Doilly, built between 1129 and 1150, stood on the same site.

CORNBURY PARK

The estate of Cornbury Park lies over the Evenlode from Charlbury. The present house is partly Tudor but mainly of the seventeenth century, and stands in the Forest of Wychwood. It is one of the greatest houses in Oxfordshire, but is private and not open to the public. The design is clearly influenced by Inigo Jones, and has an eleven-bay east front with pedimented Corinthian centrepiece, boldly projecting eaves and a stone bracket-cornice. The 1663 stables are also on a grand scale. The private chapel built in 1677 has a fine interior.

SHIPTON-UNDER-WYCHWOOD

Shipton-under-Wychwood lies on the west bank of the Evenlode and is centred around a triangular green flanked by stone cottages, the fifteenth-century Shaven Crown Inn and, on the lower side, by the church of St Mary.

Shipton Court is one of the largest Jacobean houses in England. Built in 1603, it is a much restored house overlooking terraced lawns and gardens bordered by clipped hedges, and enhanced by an ornamental pond edged by paved walkways.

FINSTOCK

Finstock lies on the southern edge of Wychwood Forest. The manor-house of 1660 has three gables and mullioned windows.

HOLY TRINITY CHURCH, ASCOTT-UNDER-WYCHWOOD

WILCOTE

Wilcote sits on the top of a hill overlooking the Evenlode. The colour-washed manor, mainly sixteenth century but mentioned in Domesday, stands close to the appealing little twelfth-century church, and a short distance away from there stands Wilcote House, a rambling stone courtyard dwelling dating from Elizabethan times, but greatly enlarged during the nineteenth century.

Wilcote Manor

NORTH LEIGH

North Leigh is a large village on a hill. The church of St Mary is one of the most interesting in the county. It has a massive Saxon tower dated between 1000 and 1050, a Norman south porch doorway, late twelfth-century nave arcades and a richly moulded tower arch with clustered shafts.

Its tour-de-force is the exquisite fan-vaulted Wilcote chapel, built in the fifteenth century. To the west a Roman villa has been excavated at Shakenoak Farm and to the east, a second-century Roman courtyard house with two sets of baths, hypocausts and mosaic pavements has been uncovered.

CHURCH HANBOROUGH

The jewel of Church Hanborough is the twelfth-century church of Saints Peter and Paul. The Norman tympanum over the north doorway is carved with St Peter with his keys, the Lion of St Mark and the cock that crowed thrice when Peter denied Christ. The nave was rebuilt in the fourteenth century, and the delicate spire is a prominent landmark down the valley. The chancel screen is pre-Reformation and in good condition, with traces of medieval blue, red and gold colouring still gleaming through.

EYNSHAM

Eynsham stands on the banks of the Thames about six miles west of Oxford. Nearby Swinford Bridge still operates a toll. The village belonged to the Anglo-Saxon kings of Mercia in the eighth century, but became prominent only when the Benedictine abbey was founded there in 1000. Sadly, no trace remains of this abbey.

Many old stone houses line the village street and, at the market square, a charming group includes an inn, the quaint little seventeenth-century Town Hall and the 20 foot high stone market cross. The church of St Leonard takes up one side of this square, and has a handsome tower of 1450 and a thirteenth-century chancel and south aisle. The Vicarage in Mill Street is of 1704 and has a five-bay front with gabled centre section.

MARKET CROSS AND TOWN HALL, EYNSHAM

Church Street, Eynsham

WITNEY

Famous for the manufacture of woollen blankets since the Middle Ages, the large market town of Witney lies just fourteen miles west of Oxford on the River Windrush. The mile-long main street winds through the town and culminates in a spacious green, at one end of which rises the imposing spire of St Mary's church. This street contains a fascinating blend of stone houses, inns, shops and factories, and at the top of the hill, close to the green, stands the Buttercross, a distinctive little building erected in 1683, with a clock turret and a sundial on its gabled roof, all supported on thirteen stone pillars.

The Blanket Hall was built in about 1721 for weighing and measuring blankets, and bears the arms of the Witney Company of Weavers. In the pediment is a clock, and on the roof, a wooden bell-turret with a cupola.

St Mary's spire dominates the landscape for miles around. Richly decorated chantry chapels have exceptional traceried windows, and the late twelfth-century porch, between the north-west chapel and the north transept, is a rare and unusual survival.

The Town Hall in the market-place is eighteenth century. The Grammar school on Church Green was founded in 1660, and is approached along a fine avenue of trees. Several elegant sixteenth- and seventeenth-century houses flank Church Green. The Fleece Hotel is Georgian, and the Angel Inn has a Georgian front. Leigh and Sons' shopfront has nineteenth-century ironwork with elaborate foliage, and J. Clarke and Sons in the High Street has intricate Victorian ironwork of 1870. The new shopping centre in Witney is in a pseudo-traditional architectural style which adds nothing to the quality of the town.

THE ANGEL, WITNEY

right THE GREEN, WITNEY

NIGEL
DIXON
&CO

THE BUTTERCROSS, WITNEY

TOLSEY MUSEUM, BURFORD

BURFORD

Nominated as the Gateway to the Cotswolds, Burford is a beautiful wool town set on the south bank of the River Windrush. The town is built up a steep hill rising from the ancient bridge and the High Street is lined with a stunning array of stone and half-timbered houses, shops and inns. At the top of the hill the street is lined with pollarded lime trees which create a dramatic approach from the south.

The church of St John the Baptist stands on the riverbank, and is one of the finest in Oxfordshire with its Norman tower and tall elegant spire. The three-storeyed pinnacled and traceried porch of 1450 is the work of a highly accomplished mason.

Some of the finest buildings in the town include the sixteenth-century Tolsey Museum, formerly a courthouse, London House, a three-storey fifteenth-century timber-framed house, Glenthorne by Kempster dated 1700 and Falkland Hall which was built in 1558. In Church Lane stand the Great Almshouses founded in 1457 by the Earl of Warwick. The Grammar School was founded in 1571 and is a long house with mullioned windows.

Other houses and inns too numerous to mention here range from the fourteenth to the eighteenth centuries, and include the former George Inn, sixteenth-century Corner House Hotel, Shoo Cottage, Bear Court, eighteenth-century Riverside House, The Old Rectory in Priory Lane, the Italianate palazzo of Great House in Witney Street and Calendars in Sheep Street, a fifteenth-century stone and half-timbered house with projecting upper floor.

TAYNTON

Taynton quarries are famous for their Oxfordshire limestone and have been worked for a thousand years. They were the source of stone for many Oxford colleges, and for Windsor Castle, Blenheim Palace and St Paul's Cathedral.

The picturesque village has stone cottages, old barns, and a late medieval church with an embattled parapet and interesting gargoyle spouts. The nave and aisles have stone corbels carved as heads, and the fifteenth-century roof has wooden bosses finely carved as pomegranate, serpent and vine.

UP HIGH STREET, BURFORD

right DOWN HIGH STREET, BURFORD

BULL
THE BULL
HOTEL

CHARTERVILLE

Some of the dwellings remain from a bold nineteenth-century resettlement project carried out by Feargus O'Connor at Charterville. His Chartist or National Land Company sought to settle families from factory houses into country smallholdings, but the scheme failed and the workers drifted back to their old homes.

SWINBROOK

Swinbrook lies in the lush meadows of the River Windrush. The church of St Mary rears up on a raised bank over the village, and is a striking building. The famous Fettiplace monuments, dating from 1613 and 1686, display six generations of the celebrated local landowners, reclining on stone and marble shelves to one side of the chancel. The family died out without issue in the eighteenth century. These monuments are amongst the most impressive and beautiful works of art in Oxfordshire, and not to be missed.

The Mitford family lived in the village and the author Nancy and her sister Unity are buried in the churchyard.

ST MARY'S CHURCH, SWINBROOK

ASTHALL

Asthall is a mellowed stone village in the Windrush valley. The Norman church of St Nicholas stands next to a beautiful 1620 manor-house.

MINSTER LOVELL

The gaunt remains of Minster Lovell Hall stand amongst the trees on the banks of the Windrush. Built in 1431, it was confiscated by the Crown in 1485, and in 1747 was dismantled.

St Kenelm's church is a cruciform fifteenth-century building with monuments to the Lovell family. A nearby barn was built in the thirteenth century.

St Nicholas' Church and the Manor Hotel, Asthall

Minster Lovell Hall Ruins

right Village Street, Minster Lovell

Minster Lovell Cottages

DUCKLINGTON VILLAGE

WIDFORD

Widford lies across the river near Swinbrook, and the remote and beautiful church of St Oswald stands on the site of a Roman villa, part of whose mosaic floor is exposed in the chancel. It has box pews and some wall paintings.

SOUTH LEIGH

South Leigh lies to the east of Witney and is notable for the remarkable wall paintings in the church of St James. These include The Last Judgement over the chancel arch, which shows St Peter greeting the saved while the lost, including a bishop and kings, are being dragged into the inferno by devils. On the south wall is the pictorially graphic Weighing of Souls, and on another wall, Pope Clement, in green and gold robes with a triple crown under a canopy.

COGGES

Cogges is now absorbed by Witney, and was the site of a medieval Benedictine priory founded in 1103. St Mary's church has an unusual fourteenth-century tower placed on the diagonal.
Manor Farm is a sixteenth-century house built on foundations of 1250, and is now a farm museum showing old implements, machinery and uncommom animal breeds.

DUCKLINGTON

Ducklington village clusters around a pond and the green. St Bartholomew's church is Transitional Norman with fine masonry details in the capitals, arches and window tracery. The 1340 north aisle is very beautiful.

STANTON HARCOURT

Stanton Harcourt lies between the Windrush and the Thames in flat water-meadows. The Harcourt family has remained in possession of the manor since 1150. During the eighteenth century, when the family had moved away temporarily, much of the medieval manor was demolished, but the Great Kitchen dating from 1380 and Pope's Tower have survived. The kitchen is one of the most complete medieval domestic examples in England, and has a remarkable octagonal pyramid roof dated 1485. Smoke escaped through the roof shutters. Pope's Tower is named after the poet Alexander Pope who stayed in it between 1717 and 1718, while translating Homer's *Iliad*. Next to the manor is the Norman and Early English church of St Michael. It contains an impressive collection of Harcourt monuments and tombs. The chancel dates from 1250 and has a trio of lancet windows divided by clustered shafts and stiff-leaf capitals. Thatched, half-timbered and stone cottages and farm buildings complete the village, which retains an uncanny atmosphere of feudal England.

STANDLAKE

Standlake is located in an area of extensive lakes and gravel workings, where birdlife and, in particular, wildfowl species such as greylag, barnacle and snow geese, can be seen in the nature reserve. The village has a half-timbered manor-house of the fifteenth and sixteenth centuries, the church of St Giles with octagonal tower and spire, and on a charming moated site, the farmhouse called Gaunt House with its fifteenth-century chimney-breast.

At the nearby junction of the Windrush and the Thames is Newbridge, a six-arch bridge over five hundred years old, with its pubs, The Rose Revived and The Maybush, situated at opposite ends.

STANTON HARCOURT MANOR

NORTHMOOR

Northmoor lies in a stretch of lush Oxfordshire countryside, a collection of stone cottages by a brook. Rectory Farm, with its barns and Tudor dovecote, stands next to the church of St Denis which has a carved wooden gallery.

COKETHORPE PARK

Cokethorpe Park was begun in 1709 for Sir Simon Harcourt. It has a pedimented west front of six bays and an Ionic porch.

THE ROSE REVIVED, NEWBRIDGE

BAMPTON

Bampton is no more than a large village now, but has some elegant Georgian houses, a market-place and a grand church crowned by a 170 foot high spire. The Italianate Town Hall of 1853 and several inns stand at the centre.

St Mary's is one of the three largest churches in Oxfordshire. There is a remarkable structural broaching transition from the octagonal spire to the square tower beneath, using corner statues linked by flying buttresses to the spire.

The old Grammar School was built between 1635 and 1653. The Deanery is a medieval building much altered in the seventeenth century. Ham Court, on the outskirts of the village, was formerly the castle with a moat and towers on each corner. Only the west gatehouse and a stretch of curtain walling remain.

CLANFIELD

Clanfield lies on the watery plain of the upper Thames between Faringdon and Witney. Small bridges across the stream, which flows the length of the village street, connect to individual houses. The church of St Stephen is Norman with many later additions. The Plough Hotel is Jacobean with a three-bay front. Friars Court was built in 1650 on the site of a Knights Templar Hospice.

KENCOT

The little church of St George in Kencot is Norman, and has a south doorway of 1150 with a tympanum showing a relief of a centaur, Sagittarius, shooting an arrow down the throat of a monster. On the green is an ancient cross, and a short distance away is Kencot House, an early eighteenth-century building of seven bays with a coved cornice, and a garden wall with a thirteenth-century arch set into it. Other notable buildings include seventeenth-century Manor Farm and Red Rose Close of 1650.

BLACK BOURTON

The manor of Black Bourton was once held by the 'black' monks of Osney Abbey. St Mary's church contains some delightful wall paintings from about 1250 and previously covered up by whitewash for four centuries. A stone house dated 1655, at the gate to the churchyard, was formerly The Horse and Groom Inn.

SHILTON

Shilton sits astride Shill Brook, where a ford creates a picturesque sight at the heart of the village. Holy Rood church stands on a hill at the south end, and has fine Norman arches and a chancel of 1250.

Manor Farm has an old dovecote with a conical roof, and Shilbon House of 1678 has a gabled three-storey projecting porch.

ST MARY'S CHURCH, BAMPTON

Village Green, Kencot

Shilton Village Street

BRIDGEWATER COTTAGE, LANGFORD

WESTWELL

Westwell is one of the most beautiful villages in Oxfordshire, having successfully resisted the twentieth century. It stands on a plateau just south of Burford and has a green and duckpond around which the old stone buildings cluster.

St Mary's church is Norman with a fine doorway of this period, and there is a very large monument to Charles Trinder and his fourteen children.

The manor-house is Tudor with sixteenth- and seventeenth-century additions.

KELMSCOTT

Kelmscott will always be associated with William Morris, the writer, artist, craftsman and social visionary, who lived in the manor. He is buried in the peaceful churchyard of St George's. The church is cruciform in plan with Transitional Norman nave and chancel dated 1190.

Kelmscott Manor stands near the Thames among barns and trees, and was built in 1570 with seventeenth-century additions. A cottage in the village shows a sculptured relief of Morris sitting under a tree in his garden.

FILKINS

Filkins lies on the Gloucestershire border south of Burford. The Cotswold Woollen Weavers have established a traditional mill opposite Filkins Hall, using ancient machinery and looms to weave fine woollen cloth, and the premises are open to the public. A museum shows local industrial and agricultural artefacts.

LANGFORD

Langford has the most remarkable Saxon building in the county. The church of St Matthew incorporates the most important remains in the south porch and central tower. The tower is entirely Saxon with the later addition of a parapet and a corbel table, and has three stages with string courses and two large bell-openings on all sides. On the two lower stages are corner pilaster strips and central pilasters with stepped Saxon capitals and bases. In 1200, aisles were added to the nave using tall round piers with carved foliage capitals and elegant round arches. Over the thirteenth-century porch door is a Saxon relief of the Crucifixion, and on the side wall a large headless sculpture of Christ with arms outstretched, dating from between the tenth and twelfth centuries.

Kelmscott Manor

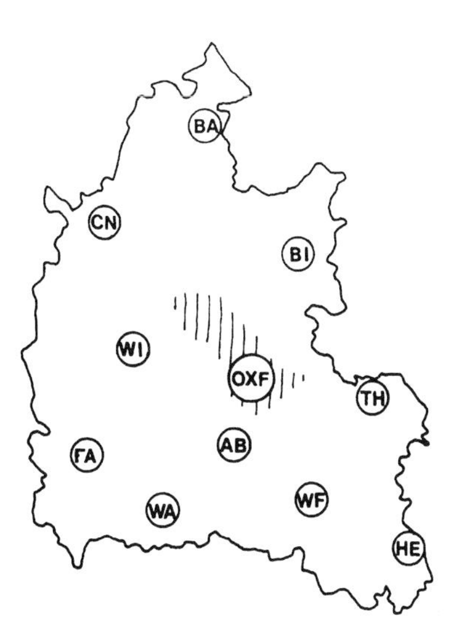

OXFORD AND BLENHEIM PALACE

At the heart of the county stands the ancient and venerated university city of Oxford. It lies in the fork of land between the Rivers Cherwell and Thames, and although it now stretches eastward in a seamless sprawl, the medieval street pattern at the centre remains largely intact. Viewed from the hills to the west, Oxford is a romantic-looking jumble of spires, domes and towers rising from the water-meadows which form its boundaries.

The city is a remarkable concentration of buildings representing every phase of English architecture over the past millennium. It proclaims its importance through its stylish buildings and commands the valley in which it sits.

Blenheim Palace is one of the great stately homes of England. As a work of architecture it is an overpowering and idiosyncratic design, but there is no disputing the grandeur of its concept and the elegance of its parkland setting.

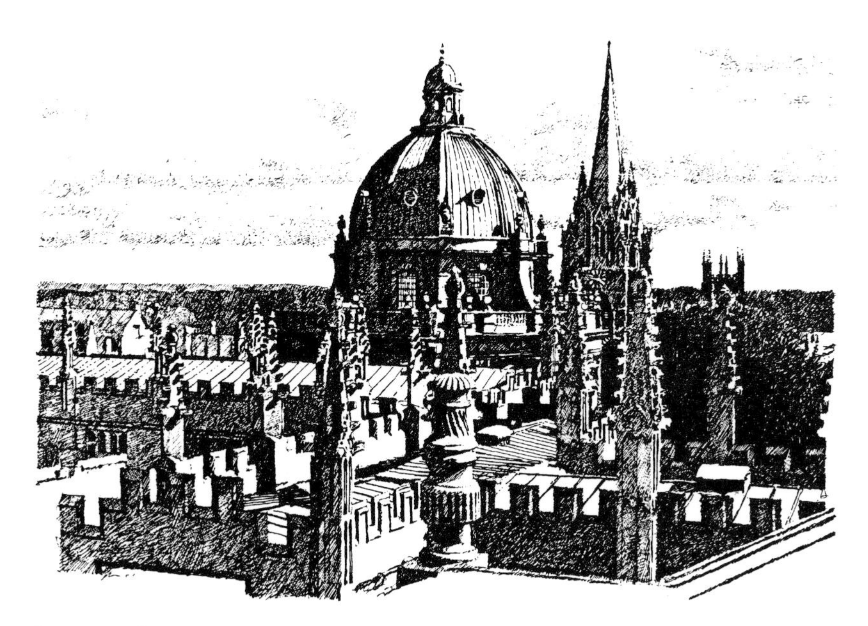

OXFORD SKYLINE

OXFORD

The Saxon princess St Frideswide built a nunnery on the site of Oxford in AD 727 and sparked the first settlement. This grew into a fortified position under Edward the Elder in the tenth century. Although the Vikings razed Oxford to the ground in 1012 it continued to grow into a flourishing centre during the Middle Ages, and William the Conqueror's governor rebuilt the walls and added a motte-and-bailey castle. By the twelfth century the city had about five thousand inhabitants and sixteen churches, and was granted a charter in 1191. The Anglo-Saxon tower of St Michael-at-the-North-Gate marks the northern limit of the medieval city and is the oldest surviving building in Oxford.

The parish church of Oxford is St Mary's, largely Perpendicular, but with a magnificent tower dating from between 1300 and 1325. For four hundred years it was used by the university for faculty and congregation meetings, and housed the University Library until 1488.

The university is the oldest in England, dating from about 1167 when expelled English scholars from the University of Paris came to Oxford in search of teachers. Merton, University, Balliol and Worcester were the first colleges to be established during the 1260s. The colleges are mostly based on inward-looking quadrangles, protected and cloistered entities which often present rather forbidding stone walls to the street. It is this pattern of building, first developed at New College by William of Wykeham in 1379, which gives Oxford its unique and particularly urban character. The medieval core of the city is compact due to its physical confinement by the rivers, and today incorporates all the civic, social and commercial functions and institutions of a cosmopolitan society. Colleges mingle with shopping streets and students with townspeople in a way that earlier generations had not experienced.

During the fourteenth century Oxford declined dramatically following the Black Death and several devastating fires. Brawls between students and citizens culminated in 1355 in a two-day street battle in which many died. After this date students lived mostly in college halls instead of town lodgings.

During the fourteenth and fifteenth centuries New College, Oriel, Queen's, Magdalen and All Souls were founded, and by the time of the dissolution of the monasteries these had been followed by Brasenose, Corpus Christi and Christ Church. Under the Reformation, monasteries and monastic colleges were suppressed, but after Oxford became a city in 1545, with twelfth-century Christ Church as its cathedral, prosperity increased and more colleges were established.

St John's and Trinity colleges were built on the accession to the throne of Mary Tudor, and followed by Jesus in 1571 and Wadham in 1610.

There was little damage during the Civil War and by the eighteenth century some of the most celebrated buildings of the city were completed or under way.

Wren designed the Sheldonian Theatre in 1667 and parts of Christ Church followed, and his pupil Nicholas Hawksmoor added All Souls' north quad and the Clarendon Building amongst others. Between them they established classical architecture at the university.

The domed Radcliffe Camera, probably the most familiar building of Oxford, was designed by Gibbs as a reading room for the Bodleian Library in 1749.

In 1882 Butterfield completed Keble College, and the first women's college, Lady Margaret Hall, was founded in 1878, although women were not admitted as full members of the university until 1920.

The twentieth century has transformed Oxford into an important industrial centre. This began with the establishment of the Morris car plant at Cowley, which led to increased population and rapid urban sprawl to the east and south of the old city.

Despite this and the pressures which such growth inevitably place upon any community, the centre of Oxford remains unspoilt and an attractive environment in which to live, work and study.

THE RADCLIFFE CAMERA

The High Street, Oxford

MAGDALEN COLLEGE

right THE SHELDONIAN THEATRE AND THE CLARENDON BUILDING

HOLYWELL STREET AND NEW COLLEGE

right ORIEL COLLEGE

ACROSS MAGDALEN BRIDGE

right MERTON STREET AND MERTON COLLEGE

BLENHEIM PALACE

Blenheim Palace lies a few miles to the north west of Oxford on the edge of the village of Woodstock, in a sumptuous parkland enhanced by lakes formed by damming of the River Glyme.

The palace was built as a national monument with funds presented by Queen Anne to John Churchill, 1st Duke of Marlborough, as a token of gratitude for the defeat of the French armies at Blenheim on the Danube in 1704. The architect was Sir John Vanbrugh, although the work was completed by his assistant, Nicholas Hawksmoor between 1705 and 1725. The park was landscaped by Capability Brown between 1764 and 1774.

Blenheim Palace is a Baroque complex of fortress-like buildings extending across high ground in the park, and is decorated with turrets, pinnacles and statues which create a distinctive silhouette. The dramatic approach from the north culminates in a gigantic forecourt to the main façade. Of nine bays, it is articulated by a giant order of Corinthian pilasters and columns.

The Great Hall is on a majestic scale and rather austere. The Saloon was decorated by Laguerre in 1720. The magnificent Long Library runs the whole length of the west front, and the chapel was completed by Hawksmoor in 1731 with monuments to John Churchill by Kent and Rysbrack. The east gardens are formal with water terraces stepping down to the lake below. The park is enriched by stands of mature trees and bold grassy slopes sweep to the horizon.

Built entirely of golden stone from the famous quarries at Taynton, Blenheim Palace is a breathtaking achievement which attracted controversy when completed, and will probably continue to draw praise and criticism but never indifference.

WOODSTOCK

Before Blenheim Palace was thought of, the manor of Woodstock was a favourite hunting lodge for English kings. Alfred the Great lived there for a time, and the Black Prince was born there in 1330.

The small town of Woodstock is an attractive place with elegant Georgian houses and shops in the High Street and several inns of which The Bear Hotel is the finest.

EAST GATE, BLENHEIM PALACE

Blenheim Palace from the Park

Forecourt and North Front, Blenheim Palace

Grand Bridge, Blenheim Park

The Bear Hotel, Market Street, Woodstock

ST LAWRENCE CHURCH, NORTH HINKSEY

BINSEY

Although part of Oxford, Binsey is a charming rural city village with a thatched inn and a tiny twelfth-century church approached down a chestnut avenue. St Margaret's Well in the churchyard marks the spot where St Frideswide prayed in her compassion when a pursuing suitor was struck blind here in the eighth century, prior to founding her nunnery.

IFFLEY

In the southern suburbs of Oxford is one of the most beautiful examples of Norman parish church building in the country. St Mary's at Iffley was built between 1154 and 1189, and had a chancel added in 1270. Both south and west doorways display some remarkably well-preserved sculpture in their arch mouldings.

BLADON

Bladon is a small village on the edge of Blenheim Park notable as the burial place of Sir Winston Churchill.

KIDLINGTON

The old part of Kidlington is down by the Cherwell. The prominent spire was known in the Middle Ages as Our Lady's Needle.

NORTH HINKSEY

The Norman church of St Lawrence at North Hinksey has an ancient stone cross in the churchyard.

WOLVERCOTE

Lower Wolvercote is a riverside village in the northern suburbs of Oxford. The scant remains of the Benedictine nunnery of Godstow lie in the meadows and across the river is the celebrated seventeenth-century Trout Inn with its weirside terrace.

CASSINGTON

The church of St Peter at Cassington was built by Geoffrey de Clinton before 1123, and has fine Norman tower arches, windows, font and sculptures. In the nave are several fifteenth-century oak benches.

next page ST MARY'S CHURCH, IFFLEY

THE VALE OF WHITE HORSE AND THE RIDGEWAY

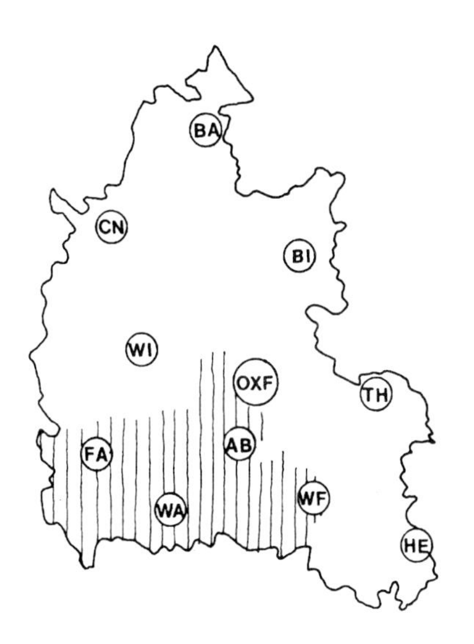

This region was once part of Berkshire and is defined by the River Thames along its northern and eastern edges and by the escarpment of the Downs to the south.

The town of Faringdon perches on the low Corallian hills which separate the Thames valley from the Vale of White Horse, and a string of picturesque villages line the ridgetop road. Where it fades to the east in the approaches to Oxford, the landscape bubbles up into a cluster of wooded hills overlooking the city.

To the south the Vale of White Horse carries the River Ock and its many tributary streams, and cradles the historic towns of Wantage and Abingdon. Strung under the escarpment of the Downs is a necklace of small villages built of chalk and timber framing.

The Downs rise dramatically to form the southern boundary of the county, and are only broken by the Thames at Goring Gap as, further east, they become the Chilterns. The ancient Icknield Way, now called The Ridgeway, holds the highest ground and commands splendid panoramic views northwards across the Vale of White Horse and beyond to the Cotswolds. The Ridgeway is steeped in pre-history, and remains are plentiful, indicating that the Downs were well-populated by successions of tribes prior to the Roman occupation.

The nineteenth century brought railways to the region, and Didcot became an important junction on the main line to the west. Didcot and the landscape for miles around are dominated by the immense and visually impressive coal-fired power station, with its six cooling towers belching plumes of steam into the Oxfordshire skies.

LONG WITTENHAM

APPLETON

Appleton lies below Cumnor Hill, west of Oxford. The church is late Norman with a four-bay north arcade of this period with round piers, square abaci and shallow capitals of leaf sculpture. There is a fine tomb to a Fettiplace Lord of the Manor.

FYFIELD

Fyfield is an attractive village with a splendid stone manor-house. Built in 1320, it retains the hall and porch to which a narrow-gabled Elizabethan wing has been added. The roof has mighty timber tie-beams, queen-post trusses and windbraces. The front is Elizabethan. Manor Farmhouse dates from 1700. The White Hart is a fifteenth-century chantry with attached priest's house founded by Sir John Golafre of the Manor.

PUSEY

Pusey is a small collection of grey stone cottages around the Georgian house built in 1753. Pusey House has fine gardens with a Chinese bridge across a lake and a temple with a dome, and the planting is spectacular.

BUCKLAND

Buckland is also on the low ridge of Corallian ragstone above the Thames. The attractive stone houses of the village group cosily near the church of St Mary, which has a cruciform plan and an impressive twelfth-century nave. The chancel roof is decorated, and there is a Jacobean pulpit with three-dimensional carving and box pews.

Buckland House was designed by Wood the Younger of Bath, and is an Italian style mansion with a five-bay main front and wings with octagonal pavilions. There is a thatched Ice House in the grounds, a rustic boathouse by the lake and a Rotunda with Ionic columns and a dome.

Radcot Bridge below Littleworth, has three ribbed arches, and is a fine fourteenth-century stone bridge. It performed a vital linking role across the Thames during the busy height of the wool trading era.

KINGSTON BAGPUIZE HOUSE

KINGSTON BAGPUIZE

Kingston Bagpuize House was built on the site of a moated Elizabethan manor-house about 1670 and is a tall brick seven-bay house with a raised pedimented centre and lower wings. Inside there is fine panelling, and a splendid staircase. The Classical church dates from 1799 to 1800 and has a cupola and a monument to Sir Edmund Fettiplace of 1710.

Buckland House

BUSCOT

Buscot is the last village on the Faringdon to Lechlade road before crossing the Thames into Gloucestershire

Buscot Park is a nine-bay, two-storey Georgian house of 1770 standing in beautiful wooded parkland.

The Old Parsonage is a beautiful two-storey Queen Anne house of 1700 standing next to the church of St Mary on the banks of the Isis.

GREAT COXWELL

Great Coxwell is celebrated for the magnificent thirteenth-century stone tithe barn which was built by Cistercian monks to hold their produce, and is the finest such building in England. The barn is over 150 feet long and 45 feet wide, and is cathedral-like in scale and structure. Its slender timber columns are supported on stone bases. Transepts and archways form entrances at opposite sides, and great doors open at each end.

FARINGDON

Faringdon was on an important crossroads for the Cotswold wool trade, and was prosperous during the fifteenth and sixteenth centuries. The market-place has a small seventeenth-century Town Hall in the middle supported on Tuscan columns, and is surrounded by shops, houses and inns. The Crown Hotel has a courtyard with a fourteenth-century range.

The church of All Saints stands on a rise to one side and has a Norman nave with a thirteenth-century chancel and a tower added in 1645, following destuction by cannon-balls during the Civil War. Interesting monuments range from the fourteenth to the seventeenth centuries.

Faringdon House stands north of the church, and is a five-bay, two-storey stone and stuccoed building completed in 1780. Lord Berners lived here during the 1930s, and built a strange brick tower as a folly in 1935.

MARKET HOUSE, FARINGDON

right THE OLD PARSONAGE, BUSCOT

ST PETER'S CHURCH, CHARNEY BASSETT

left GREAT COXWELL TITHE BARN

STANFORD-IN-THE-VALE

Stanford-in-the-Vale was an important market centre up to the sixteenth-century when neighbouring Wantage and Faringdon began to overshadow it.

The large church of St Denys is impressive and has some fine Decorated and Perpendicular window tracery.

There are some elegant and substantial houses around the two greens in the village, including Manor Farmhouse with its 1618 barn, eighteenth-century Rectory House, Penstone's Farmhouse and Coxe's Hall, built in 1733 with a brick Georgian front.

CHARNEY BASSETT

Charney Bassett lies north of Wantage in the Vale of White Horse. The church of St Peter stands next to the manor-house. It has some excellent Norman carving in the south doorway, the outer moulding displaying faces with forked tongues sticking out, and a tympanum showing a man holding two gryphons and being bitten by them.

WEST HANNEY

West Hanney lies in the flat countryside of the Vale of White Horse looking southwards to the rising escarpments of the Downs beyond Wantage. West Hanney House of 1727 is a six-bay, two-storey building with a raised centre and curved parapets sweeping up to it.

HARWELL

Harwell is famous for the Atomic Energy Research Establishment sited two miles from the village. There are several timbered houses and thatched dwellings close to the church, which is late Norman, and has a fine fourteenth-century chancel and a pre-Reformation screen.

STEVENTON

Steventon has a unique mile-long raised causeway, built by Benedictine monks about 1300, to provide a dry path for visitors to the priory and church in times of flood. The priory is a timber-framed house with projecting gables and a sixteenth-century hall. The solar wing is late fourteenth century with a king-post roof.

Several fine timber-framed sixteenth- and seventeenth-century houses line one side of The Causeway. The church of St Michael is mainly of the early fourteenth-century.

THE CAUSEWAY, STEVENTON

ABINGDON TOWN HALL

ABINGDON

Abingdon became famous for cloth manufacture in the late Middle Ages, and has since added brewing, flour milling and agricultural machinery production. The 1416 bridge across the River Ock is the entrance into the town from the south. The bustling market-place is dominated by the towering Town Hall built in 1678 by Kempster, a pupil of Christopher Wren. This magnificent Renaissance building now contains a museum in the former Assize Court on the first floor.

The only remains of the important Benedictine abbey founded here in AD 675 are the fifteenth-century gateway attached to St Nicholas's church, and a granary and kitchen block down by the river. Nothing remains of the Abbey church.

The old town centre is an attractive network of historic streets such as East St Helen's Street, leading to St Helen's church and a remarkable group of almshouses. Christ's Hospital Almshouses were founded in 1446, and its dwelling units are connected by a long wooden cloister bordering the churchyard.

The church has a prominent thirteenth-century steeple and the building was greatly enlarged during the fifteenth and sixteenth centuries. The panelled roof in the north aisle was painted in 1390.

Other notable buildings include Tritty's Almshouses of 1707, Brick Alley Almshouses of 1718, Stratton House of 1722, mid-sixteenth-century The Gables, The Knowl with its timber-framed oversailing upper floor, and The Lion Inn in the High Street.

CUMNOR

Cumnor was the scene of the mysterious death of Robert Dudley's wife, Amy Robsart. Dudley, the Earl of Leicester, was Queen Elizabeth's favourite, and lived at Cumnor Place. It was rumoured that he had organized Amy's death so that he could be free to marry the Queen, but this was never proved.

The Norman church of St Michael has thirteenth-century arcades and a two-decker Jacobean pulpit. The stalls have poppyheads and there is a white stone statue of Queen Elizabeth in the church. The 1685 timber spiral staircase under the tower is another remarkable feature of this church.

The Bear and Ragged Staff is a solid sixteenth- and seventeenth-century inn with gables, mullioned windows and engaging interiors. The present three-arch bridge at Swinford was built in 1777 on the site of a medieval predecessor.

WYTHAM

Wytham lies just outside Oxford, and consists of thatched stone cottages, the White Hart Inn, and Wytham Abbey with its Tudor front and seven hundred acre park.

During the eighth century the Mercian king, Offa, had a house here. A small door from Cumnor Place gains entry to the churchyard of All Saints, which was largely rebuilt in 1810 by Lord Abingdon.

MARCHAM

Marcham belonged to the Abbey of Abingdon, and the remains of a priory stand just half a mile to the south east. A rectangular range has mullioned windows and sixteenth-century lights, and the hall is divided by a fireplace which opens into both.

CHRIST'S HOSPITAL ALMSHOUSES, ABINGDON

All Saints Church Tower, Sutton Courtenay

LITTLE WITTENHAM

Little Wittenham is tucked in the lee of the Wittenham Clumps, on one of which a Romano-British fort was built to command the river approach. A footpath crosses the river at Day's Lock to link with Dorchester.

BRIGHTWELL-CUM-SOTWELL

Brightwell-cum-Sotwell has a Georgian three-storey manor and some pretty thatched cottages near the church of St Agatha, the tower of which was added in 1797.

SUTTON COURTENAY

The fascinating large village of Sutton Courtenay has a gabled Manor House with a thirteenth-century hall range, a house known as the Abbey, built by Abingdon monks in the fourteenth century, and a Norman house opposite the church which has been occupied for over eight hundred years.

The main street is long and partially tree-lined, and widens at the centre near the church of All Saints which has Norman details , but whose most interesting feature is the unusual brick porch. Eric Blair, whose writing name was George Orwell, is buried in the churchyard. Other interesting buildings include Buckridges of 1631 with gables and oriels, 1820 almshouses, eighteenth-century Courtenay Lodge, nineteenth-century Mill House, and Goslings, a timber-framed house in Drayton Road.

MILTON

The Manor at Milton is a tall brick mansion of five bays and three storeys built between 1660 and 1670, and reputedly to the designs of Inigo Jones. It has an impressive oak staircase and some fine rooms including the library and the chapel on the first floor. The church is Victorian and dedicated to St Blaise, the patron saint of woolcombers.

LONG WITTENHAM

Long Wittenham lies along the banks of the Thames, the mile-long village street containing many attractive timbered and plastered houses. The church stands behind part-medieval Church Farm, and has a Norman chancel arch and an outstanding eight-hundred-year-old lead font decorated with flower and wheel designs and a row of bishops. In the base of the piscina is a tiny seven-hundred-year-old stone figure of a knight, the smallest sculptured monument in the land.

The Barley Mow Inn has three bays of cruck construction.

House in Milton Road, Sutton Courtenay

RECTORY COTTAGE, DIDCOT

DIDCOT

Didcot is on the main-line railway junction to Oxford, and it was the railway itself which led to the siting of the massive coal-fired power station to the north west of the town. The cooling towers are colossal, and can be seen from the Downs, the Cotswolds and the Chilterns, as they expel their billowing plumes of steam into the atmosphere.

The old part of the town has a few timber-framed houses near the church of All Saints which has a timber bell-turret and shingled spire. A marble effigy of the thirteenth-century Abbot of Abingdon, Ralph de Dudecote, stands inside.

NORTH MORETON

North Moreton church of All Saints possesses the finest medieval stained glass of any village church in Oxfordshire. Almost seven hundred years old, the colours still glow richly from the south chapel east window, illustrating scenes from the life of Christ, the Virgin, St Nicholas, St Peter and St Paul.

The village has some seventeenth-century timbered buildings and a pub called The Bear, with its inn sign depicting Rupert the cartoon character. Cobbs Cottage has two gables and an oriel window.

ASTON UPTHORPE

Aston Upthorpe adjoins Aston Tirrold, but has its own separate church with a window dedicated to St Birinus. The eighteenth-century Presbyterian chapel was an early meeting-house for Nonconformists. Looming over both villages is Blewburton Hill, an Iron Age hill-fort.

EAST HAGBOURNE

Although desperately close to the sprawl of Didcot, East Hagbourne remains separate and is one of the most attractive villages in the county. The main street straggles between lovely timber-framed houses with overhanging upper floors, and the stream seems ever-present. St Andrew's church has a thirteenth-century arcade and a twelfth-century chancel arch supported by carved grinning faces. Coscote Manor is a seventeenth-century timber-framed house on the road to West Hagbourne.

BLEWBURY

The village of Blewbury is roughly square, with a brook flowing through the middle. The church of St Michael stands in the centre and is Norman, with a rib-vaulted chancel and a beautiful medieval door to the rood loft. Timbered buildings, thatched cottages and old cob walls abound. The Downs rise out of the village to Churn Knob where St Birinus is supposed to have preached the gospel to the people of Wessex during the seventh century.

East Hagbourne Village Street

WALLINGFORD TOWN HALL

MOULSFORD

Sited on one of the most beautiful stretches of the Thames, Moulsford has a simple Victorian church on the river bank, and a popular hostelry called The Beetle and Wedge surveying the passing boat traffic. The Downs sweep up behind the village through woodlands to the Ridgeway and the Berkshire border.

CHOLSEY

Cholsey lies south of Wallingford in flat Thames countryside. St Mary's is a major Norman cruciform church of flint and stone built by the monks of Reading Abbey. Enormous Norman arches support the central tower.

Manor Farm once had the largest barn in England until demolition in 1815, and the present structure was built with reused material from it.

WALLINGFORD

Wallingford is sited at an important Thames crossing. In the eleventh century William the Conqueror commissioned the building of a castle to guard the crossing, and this lasted until just after the Civil War. Only grass-covered mounds remain.

Chartered by Henry II in 1155, Wallingford grew into an attractive market town, and by 1670 had a Town Hall, several inns including The White Hart, The Lamb and The George, and many fine town houses. The bridge had three arches built in the thirteenth century and the remaining arches were added during the eighteenth century. St Mary's church is a large 1854 flint building. St Leonard's is Norman.

Other buildings of note include the Corn Exchange in the market-place, an Italianate stone edifice of 1856, an Elizabethan brick and pargeted house called St Lucian's, and the Augiers almshouses of 1681.

VILLAGE STREET, EAST HENDRED

left THE THAMES AT WALLINGFORD

WANTAGE

Wantage was well established by the seventh century, and was the birthplace, in 849, of King Alfred, self-styled King of the English, and known as Alfred the Great. A statue of him stands in the market-place. During the Middle Ages, Wantage grew around its market, which flourishes still. The church of St Peter and St Paul is a large cruciform building dating from the thirteenth century, and has lovely medieval choir stalls with carved misericords. The market-place has several fine eighteenth-century buildings along its south side including The Bear Hotel. Style's Almshouses were built in 1680. King Alfred's School was founded in the reign of Queen Elizabeth I.

LOCKINGE

Lockinge is a charming model estate village just east of Wantage, and has a church with Norman details and a tower of 1564.

ARDINGTON

Ardington lies just off the Roman Portway and is an attractive group of houses, school, rectory and inn around the squat church of Holy Trinity. Georgian Ardington House is a three-storey brick building with a centre bay carrying a decorated pediment, and was erected in 1721.

WEST HENDRED

The fourteenth-century church of West Hendred is by Ginge Brook, which tumbles from the nearby Downs. Fragments of old glass include an inscription, 'C Parker glazed this church and glad of the job 1784'.

EAST HENDRED

The extremely picturesque village of East Hendred lies at the foot of the Downs, a wide main street lined with brick and timber-framed houses.

Hendred House is a medieval manor belonging to the Eyston family, who have been there since 1450, and contains a thirteenth-century chapel.

King's Manor is a good timber-framed house, and the Jesus chapel has a fifteenth-century framed priest's house attached.

Opposite the manor is the church of St Augustine of Canterbury, with its thirteenth-century arches and carved wooden lectern and screens. The faceless clock, built by John Seymour in 1525, is one of the oldest in England in original working order.

King Alfred's Statue, Wantage

ARABELLA'S COTTAGE, LETCOMBE BASSETT

WEST CHALLOW

West Challow is remote, although only about two miles from the centre of Wantage. The church of St Lawrence possesses the oldest bell in England, made in 1283. Manor Farm has a fine early eighteenth-century front in blue and red brick.

SPARSHOLT

Sparsholt is overlooked by the Downs which rise up to 700 feet near the Devil's Punchbowl. The church of Holy Cross is Norman with a thirteenth-century tower and fourteenth-century chancel. The north door has late twelfth-century iron scrollwork, and some rare and beautiful carved wooden effigies of a fourteenth-century knight and two wives.

CHILDREY

Childrey is a charming village of brick and half-timbered cottages lining the green and the prominent pond. St Mary's church is a splendid mainly fourteenth-century building. The great local landowners, the Fettiplaces, lived here until about 1500 when they moved to Swinbrook. The transepts were endowed as chantry chapels by the De Chilrey and Fettiplace families. The remarkable Norman font has a frieze of lead bishops.

LETCOMBE REGIS

Letcombe Regis is a large village with modern houses mixed in with the old. Regis cottage is a fine half-timbered house near the church of St Andrew which itself has some good glass fragments.

LETCOMBE BASSETT

The extremely picturesque village of Letcombe Bassett stands fairly high up on the side of the Downs. A brook with watercress beds has cut a deep valley along one edge of the village, and cottages perch on the bank above it. One thatched dwelling is named Arabella's Cottage after a Thomas Hardy character in *Jude the Obscure*. The church has a Norman doorway and a tiny chancel arch of the same period. Iron Age sherds and a Saxon burial place have been discovered at the hill-fort on Segsbury Down, directly above the village.

ST MARY'S CHURCH, UFFINGTON

left THE VILLAGE POND, CHILDREY

WOOLSTONE

Walfric's tun, or Woolstone, lies below White Horse hill. Old cottages assemble near the quaint sixteenth-century White Horse Inn, and next to Manor farm stands the Norman church of All Saints with its lead font and carved north doorway.

KINGSTON LISLE

Kingston Lisle is tucked under the Downs, in the stretch of enchanting countryside lining the southern fringe of the Vale of White Horse. There are stands of fine trees in the grounds of Kingston Lisle House, a Georgian and Regency house with an eccentric flying staircase.

The church of St John the Baptist has a nave of 1200 and a Norman chancel. In the east window jambs are paintings of St Peter and St Paul, and elsewhere, of Salome doing a somersault before Herod. The Blowing Stone is on the road up to the Downs, and is rumoured to have been used by King Alfred as a trumpet to summon his troops against the Danes. Legends are powerful in these parts.

ASHBURY

Ashbury lies on a slope of the Downs against the Wiltshire border. Its chalk and thatched cottages cluster tightly below the fifteenth-century manor-house and the church of St Mary. Climbing out of the village to the south the road reaches the top of the Downs where the Ridgeway footpath crosses it. Not far to the east is Wayland's Smithy, a prehistoric chamber tomb flanked by sarsen stones in a clump of majestic beech trees. Continuing along the road, it reaches Ashdown House, a seventeenth-century hunting lodge built for the Earl of Craven. The house is tall with a hipped roof and a central cupola, and has low wings on each side.

COMPTON BEAUCHAMP

Compton Beauchamp consists of the Manor, a moated Tudor brick building with a stone Georgian wing, a rectory and the tiny chalk-built church of St Swithun which perches on the rise.

UFFINGTON

Uffington church is large and impressive and known as the Cathedral of the Vale. Built in the thirteenth century, it has a crossing tower with octagonal upper stages, part of which dates from 1740.

The tiny chalk-built Uffington school of 1617 was attended by Thomas Hughes, the author of *Tom Brown's Schooldays*, who was born and brought up here.

The White Horse is situated about a mile south of the village on the top of the Downs. It is one of England's most famous prehistoric landmarks and its 360 foot long white chalk-cut image of a horse has puzzled historians trying to determine its origin. Some believe that it is the work of Belgic tribesmen who settled on these hills during the first century AD.

The Iron Age hill fort known as Uffington Castle stands nearby, and from here there are magnificent views to be enjoyed across the Vale.

left WAYLAND'S SMITHY

ST SWITHUN'S CHURCH, COMPTON BEAUCHAMP

ASHDOWN HOUSE, ASHBURY

THE THAME, THE CHILTERNS AND THE THAMES VALLEY

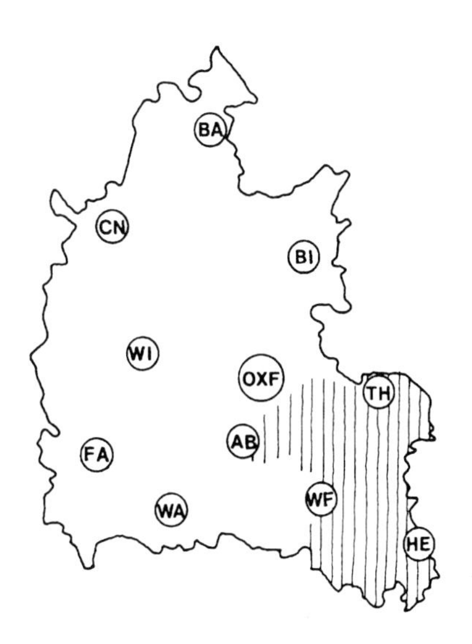

Most of Oxfordshire is taken up by farmland, but here in the south-eastern quarter the Chiltern Hills bestride the landscape in a richly sculpted terrain of beech-lined chalk ridges and wooded spurs, interwoven with green valleys and secluded combes. Settlements are made up of small farmsteads, cottages and an occasional inn, and are sprinkled over an intricate web of twisting lanes.

At the southern fringes of the hills, along the banks of the Thames which loops majestically around to form the boundary with Berkshire, Henley, Shiplake, Whitchurch and Goring draw to them the main concentrations of population, creating a string of elegant riverside towns, which have blossomed as commuter retreats since Edwardian times.

Between Goring Gap and Mapledurham is one of the most seductive stretches of the Thames, a passage of smooth reflective waters sliding peacefully beneath steep tree-covered banks on the Oxfordshire side, and past gently rising downland slopes on the opposite shore.

The escarpments of the beech-clad Chilterns are dramatically abrupt on their north western flanks, creating sudden penetrating vistas across the plain towards Oxford and Thame.

The northern half of the region lies in the valley of the River Thame, and is contrastingly flat, but nonetheless interesting, as it contains the beautiful market town of Thame itself. Other features of this area are Rycote chapel, the striking medieval group of church, almshouses and school at Ewelme, the ancient abbey church at Dorchester, and the cosy little town of Watlington.

There are great country houses at Stonor Park, Thame Park, Mapledurham and Nuneham Courtenay, and lesser but equally fine houses include Haseley Court at Little Haseley, moated thirteenth-century Shirburn Castle, Grey's Court at Rotherfield Greys and seventeenth-century Newington House.

As the home of the world famous regatta, Henley-on-Thames has a special place in English hearts, and stands on a sublime tree-lined reach of the river, with its flamboyant Victorian boathouses and stylish eighteenth-century inns spread along the town bank close to the five-arch bridge.

CHILTERN BEECHES

DORCHESTER

Dorchester is the most historic settlement in Oxfordshire. By the end of the fourth century AD it was a Roman garrison camp guarding the Thames crossing. In AD 635 the Benedictine monk Birinus baptized the King of Wessex in the Thame and, as St Birinus, founded a church here as the Cathedral of Wessex, one of the early shrines of Christianity. After the Norman Conquest, the bishopric was transferred to Lincoln, and the Augustinians built the Abbey church we see today. In 1536 the monastic buildings were demolished under the Dissolution.

The abbey is cruciform in plan. The north wall is original, and a north aisle was added in the thirteenth century. In 1340 the choir was extended eastwards, and it is here that the remarkable windows are to be seen. The east window fills the end wall, and the north wall is the Jesse Window, its tracery carved with foliage forming a Tree of Life springing from the recumbent figure of Jesse on the sill. Figures of Christ's ancestors, the Angel Gabriel and the three wise men appear in the branches. On the south window transome bar stand six stone figures of saints and monks carrying the bier of St Birinus. The piscina and sedilia are magnificently canopied with crocketed spirelets over rib-vaults. The canopies have crocketed gables with small figures of saints. The lead font is one of the best preserved in England. The stained glass in the chancel is exceptional and dates from between 1290 and 1320. The lych-gate was designed in 1852 by Butterfield.

Other notable buildings in Dorchester include The George Inn, with its shambling gabled front, jettied first floor and arched carriageway; the fourteenth- to fifteenth-century Old School House which was the abbey guesthouse converted in 1654; the early sixteenth-century manor-house; seventeenth-century Rotten Row; the priory beside the abbey gateway with its Georgian front; The White Hart of 1691 in timber framing, brick and stucco; several thatched cottages in Malthouse Lane; Watling Lane Cottage, a sixteenth-century thatched half-timbered house; Late Georgian Willoughby House and many thatched and timbered cottages.

VILLAGE STREET, DORCHESTER

Abbey Gateway, Dorchester

High Street and The George Inn, Dorchester

CASTLE CLOSE AND THE CASTLE HOTEL, BENSON

BENSON

Benson has two grand eighteenth-century inns, The Castle and The White Hart. The church of St Helen has a medieval nave incorporating Norman, Early English and Decorated details, and a Georgian tower of 1765 to complete the picture.

BERRICK SALOME

The name Berrick Salome derives from Old English 'berewic', meaning 'barley farm', and a Norman family name, Suleham. The tiny church of St Helen has a timber-framed tower and an internal wooden gallery dated 1676.

NEWINGTON

Newington has a fine twelfth-century church with a thirteenth-century spire and sanctus bell. Next to the church, Newington House is an imposing square stone building dated 1664 with a forecourt and gateway. A third storey was added in 1777.

DRAYTON ST LEONARD

Drayton stands in a flat landscape between the Thame and the Thames. St Leonard's church has a Norman nave and a fifteenth-century timber-framed tower. The chancel is paved with ancient floor tiles. Waterside House is of the fifteenth century with a tithe barn of the same date.

CLIFTON HAMPDEN

Clifton Hampden huddles beside the Thames where a long seven-arch brick bridge, designed by George Gilbert Scott, spans the river. The church of St Michael, also by Scott, perches on a small cliff overlooking the river. There are several idyllic looking thatched cottages and The Plough Inn is of cruck construction.

left THATCHED COTTAGES, CLIFTON HAMPDEN

CHURCH AND COTTAGES, CLIFTON

NUNEHAM COURTENAY

Built astride the Oxford to Henley road, the model village of Nuneham Courtenay was completed in 1764 by Earl Harcourt, who had demolished the old village surrounding the manor.

Nuneham Park was landscaped by Capability Brown with wooded slopes falling to the river. The house is a confused amalgam of designs by several architects, including Leadbetter, Brown, Holland and Smirke, but nevertheless has some fine interiors. It is no longer the seat of the Harcourts who have returned to Stanton Harcourt.

MARSH BALDON

Marsh Baldon is a mixture of old and modern houses and farms around a spacious green crossed by a stream, and shaded by some grand trees. St Peter's church has an octagonal tower built about 1300. Baldon House has an early seventeenth-century façade with three gables and a projecting two-storey porch.

GARSINGTON

Garsington lies only two miles from the Oxford ring road, but retains a village atmosphere. The stone manor-house is Tudor with seventeenth-century additions, and has a gabled front and a forecourt framed by high yew hedges.

The church of St Mary stands on high ground looking across towards the Chilterns. The tower is of 1200 and the arcades are of the thirteenth century.

CUDDESDON

Cuddesdon sits on top of a steep hill east of Cowley, and is fortunately screened from it. The church of All Saints once belonged to Abingdon Abbey and dates from 1180. It has a cruciform plan and a central tower. The west porch entrance is an impressive fourteenth-century design, and the south porch is Norman.

ALL SAINTS CHURCH, CUDDESDON

GRANNY'S COTTAGE, CHALGROVE

GREAT MILTON

Great Milton lies close to the Thame and has a green, two old inns, The Bull and The Bell, and many thatched cottages. The manor-house has a wing of 1600 and a fifteenth-century central hall. It is now used as a restaurant. The Great House was built in 1720 and has a seven-bay front and a doorcase with fluted Doric pilasters.

The priory has a sixteenth-century façade of three gables with mullioned windows, and arms to the Boyle family over the entrance. St Mary's church has thirteenth-century arcades but was rebuilt after a fire by G.G. Scott in 1850. The Dormer monument of 1616 is an impressive alabaster tomb, and one of the finest in Oxfordshire.

STADHAMPTON

The spacious green at Stadhampton is fringed by old houses, a seventeenth-century manor-house and the church of St John the Baptist with its Georgian tower and urn-shaped corner finials.

CHISELHAMPTON

Over the eight-arch sixteenth-century Thame bridge from Stadhampton lies Chiselhampton, a small hamlet with a neat Georgian church built in 1762, and complete with high box pews and a gallery on Tuscan columns. Chiselhampton House of 1768 is a plain brick building with stone pilasters and an Ionic porch. Camoys Court is a seventeenth-century moated farmhouse incorporating a fourteenth-century house.

CHALGROVE

Chalgrove is a modern village with only the church of St Mary, with its medieval interior and chancel wall paintings, and a few old houses alongside the stream, to indicate its origins. Manor Farm is a fifteenth-century timber-framed house, and Langley Hall an early sixteenth-century house with a stuccoed Georgian façade.

LITTLE HASELEY

Haseley Court at Little Haseley is a medieval house remodelled during the eighteenth century with a seven-bay wing dated 1710. Part of the fourteenth to fifteenth century house is in a two-storey wing adjoined to the main block and, on its north side, the gable is stepped. The gardens are spectacular, with clipped yew hedges set in a formal layout to the east. Cottage pavilions with hipped roofs form a quaint closing building to a garden courtyard on the north.

GREAT HASELEY

Great Haseley is a charming village of thatched, timber-framed and stone cottages, a seventeenth-century manor-house with a Georgian stable block, a fifteenth-century tithe barn, and the Old Rectory with its fifteenth-century hall, where Christopher Wren was rector before the Commonwealth. St Peter's church is an impressive Norman and Early English building.

BRIGHTWELL BALDWIN

Brightwell Baldwin lies west of Watlington. Brightwell Park has many fine old trees and a spring flowing through it, but the Georgian house was demolished, leaving only the stable block and a seventeenth-century dovecote.

The church is mainly fourteenth century with monuments to the Stone family, and some good fifteenth-century stained glass. The Lord Nelson Inn opposite has a wooden veranda to the road and gabled projecting wings. Glebe Farm is a thatched, timber-framed house with herringbone-brick infilling.

LEWKNOR

Church Farm has a remarkable barn with a massive aisled timber structure dating from the late fourteenth century.

St Margaret's church has a Norman structure. The piscina, sedilia, a tomb recess and a priest's door all have elaborate crocketed canopies and finials. The little 1836 tiled and thatched school stands just outside the churchyard.

ST BARTHOLOMEW'S CHURCH, BRIGHTWELL BALDWIN

Haseley Court, Little Haseley

THAME

Thame has been a market town since the thirteenth century, and its mile-long street is lined with old inns and houses in a fascinating variety of styles and materials from different periods.

The earlier fifteenth- and sixteenth-century buildings are timber-framed and gabled. The Georgian fronts have spectacular controlled brickwork in red, yellow, silver-grey and blue, and elegantly proportioned windows.

In 1950 the market was moved from the wide central part of Thame to one end of the street, shifting the natural centre of gravity which rests in front of the Jacobean style Town Hall.

St Mary's church is offset at the north end of the High Street close to the river, and is a large cruciform thirteenth-century building with many interesting monuments and brasses.

In Church Lane are a sixteenth-century brick and half-timber barn, the Old Grammar School of 1558 to 1569, and half-timbered almshouses of 1550 with an overhanging gable facing the High Street.

Along the High Street itself, The Spread Eagle is a beautiful red and blue brick hotel of 1740, with a five-bay front defined by pilasters and moulded brick details.

The Bird Cage is a tower-like gabled fifteenth-century timber-framed inn, with oriels and original fireplaces on the first floor. The Saracen's Head has a fifteenth-century vault in the cellar.

A mile to the south of Thame lies Thame Park. Built on the site of a Cistercian abbey founded in 1138, the present house incorporates only the early sixteenth-century abbot's lodgings. It has two main façades, one Georgian, the other Gothic. The south range is extremely attractive with battlemented bay windows and stair turrets, and a steeply pitched roof, all dating from about 1500. The Abbot's Parlour was decorated in the Italian Renaissance style between 1530 and 1539, and has linenfold panelling, a plain stone fireplace and a recess into the oriel window. A deep frieze of panels is carved with a filigree pattern of arabesques, mermaids, scrolls and urns framing shields.

RYCOTE CHAPEL

The Perpendicular chapel at Rycote was built as a chantry in 1449 by Richard Quartermayne. It is renowned for its sumptuous seventeenth-century fittings including two canopied pews, one of which is domed, and for the splendid wagon-vaulted roof. A spiral staircase at the west end leads up to priests' rooms where there are spy windows to the chapel.

The two large pews which stand either side of the central aisle are square screened rooms decorated with fretwork and carved timberwork. The dome over the royal pew is painted on the underside with stars on a blue background, and the family pew has an upper storey approached by wooden stairs.

In the chapel yard is an ancient yew tree, reputedly planted to commemorate the coronation of King Stephen in 1135. Fragments of the great Tudor mansion are incorporated into the present house which stands next to the chapel.

THE BIRDCAGE, THAME

Cruke Cottage, Thame

Rycote Chapel

CAMILLA COTTAGE, WATERSTOCK

TOWERSEY

Towersey stands in flat country on the Buckinghamshire border, and is an attractive village around a crossroads with greens, farms and a pond. St Catherine's church is mainly of the fourteenth century.

EMMINGTON

The tiny farming hamlet of Emmington is on a cul-de-sac lane. The simple early fourteenth-century church of St Nicholas, which has now closed after seven hundred years of worship, has a saddleback tower roof and stands alone in a field.

CHINNOR

The mostly modern village of Chinnor is tucked under Bledlow Ridge with its great beech woods. St Andrew's church is a high thirteenth-century structure and has a remarkable collection of brasses and pre-Reformation glass.

SYDENHAM

Sydenham is a well-kept small village with some thatched cottages and a church with a wooden central tower and iron broach spire. Ryder's Farm is an eighteenth-century brick building with dormers and octagonal window panes.

ASTON ROWANT

Aston Rowant church has a Norman nave, fourteenth- and fifteenth-century additions, a thirteenth-century Purbeck marble font and a colourful Elizabethan monument to Lady Cecil Hobbes.

WATERSTOCK

Waterstock stands against the River Thame, five miles to the west of Thame itself. The church of St Leonard was begun in the fifteenth century, and rebuilt in 1790 before Street carried out a sensitive restoration in 1858. There are several pretty thatched cottages in the village including Camilla Cottage.

THE WAYS, CHINNOR

Barn End Cottage, Sydenham

SHIRBURN CASTLE

Shirburn has a small thirteenth- and fourteenth-century church standing just outside the grounds of the castle. The moated brick castle has a quadrangular plan with corner towers, and was built as a fortress in about 1377 by Warca de Lisle, with a gatehouse and drawbridge on the north-west side. It is a private house and not open to the public.

WATLINGTON

Watlington lies at the foot of the Chiltern escarpment, and is an attractive market town whose market was granted in 1252. It has only three principal streets and some winding lanes, and focuses on the Town Hall, an imposing 1665 brick building with an open ground floor, which once served as both grammar school and covered market. There are many fine Georgian and Victorian houses and shopfronts, and a Wesleyan chapel built in 1812 of chequered brick with arched doorways. Watlington Hill climbs up to Christmas Common, from where great long views can be had from the ridge and from Watlington Park.

BRITWELL SALOME

Britwell Salome lies at the foot of Britwell Hill, which leads up to the Ridgeway, or Icknield Way. The small rebuilt church lies behind Priory Farm, where twenty-five nuns sheltered from the French Revolution. Britwell House is an elegant brick house on a Palladian plan with a pedimented centre linked by curved walls to square wing pavilions.

SWYNCOMBE

Swyncombe is enfolded by the delectable beech woods and slopes of the Chilterns. St Botolph's church is a small Early English building of flint and stone. Swyncombe House is a modern replacement for earlier sixteenth- and nineteenth-century houses, and sits well in its stunning landscape environment.

TOWN HALL, WATLINGTON

Shirburn Castle

Swyncombe House and The Chilterns

STONOR PARK

STONOR

Stonor lies in an unspoilt and remote valley in the Chilterns, hemmed in by steep-sided wooded hills. The small village has flint and brick cottages, and White Pond Farm has a fine timber-framed barn.

Stonor Park is one of the finest houses in Oxfordshire and is built up against the hillside on the site of earlier dwellings. The straggling medieval house was remodelled in the sixteenth century and again in the eighteenth century. The beautiful brickwork, some of which is the work of Flemish craftsmen, dates from 1416 to 1760. Part of the walling from the original house of 1190 survives, but in the fourteenth century the house was greatly enlarged, and by the late fifteenth century it would have enclosed three sides of a courtyard.

Remodelled between 1534 and 1540 by Sir Walter Stonor, Sir Francis Stonor then completed the porch and created the library and long gallery from earlier rooms between 1753 and 1760. Thomas Stonor remodelled the interior, and erected the present front over fifteen bays with sash windows. During the Reformation, Edmund Campion went into hiding at Stonor Park.

The attached eleventh-century Chapel of the Holy Trinity, extensively added to in the fourteenth century, is built of flint and stone, and is a simple hall with a brick tower built in 1416, and remodelled in the late eighteenth century with a Gothic pyramidal roof and a Georgian wooden lantern. The Stonor family still lives in the house, which is open to the public during the summer.

NETTLEBED

Once the centre of the local brick-making industry, Nettlebed has only one remaining kiln preserved in the village as a monument. There are some attractive eighteenth-century houses, the early Georgian Bull Inn and the seventeenth-century White Hart. The Working Men's Club of 1912 is an Arts and Crafts Movement building around three sides of a courtyard.

BIX

The old church of Bix was abandoned in 1875 and lies overgrown alongside the steep lane leading to Maidensgrove.

Stonor Park

HART STREET, HENLEY-ON-THAMES

SHIPLAKE

Shiplake is in lovely countryside rising above the Thames just south of Henley, and stands on a ridge overlooking the river meadows. The church has medieval remnants built into a restoration in 1869 by Street. Shiplake House is a five-bay, three-storey stuccoed house of 1830. The White House of 1908 is in art nouveau style with bowed wrought-iron verandas.

HENLEY-ON-THAMES

Henley commands a beautiful stretch of water on the Thames, and is renowned for its great annual regatta. The approach to Henley from London is dramatic as the road dips sharply through the woods on Remenham Hill and crosses the five-arch bridge into the town.

The dominant tower of St Mary's church rises behind the old inns on the river bank, creating a memorable composition. At the river crossing there was a twelfth-century settlement which became a river port for the supply of timber, corn and malt to London.

During the eighteenth century Henley became a coaching halt between London and Oxford and much rebuilding followed. The railway arrived in 1857 causing further expansion, and the M4 motorway has turned it into a commuter town.

Hart Street and Market Street lead from the bridge to the Town Hall, and are lined with elegant Georgian buildings whose façades often mask earlier construction behind.

The Old White Hart is a fifteenth- and sixteenth-century inn with a rear courtyard, original timber-framing, and a projecting upper floor reached by an external staircase.

The Catherine Wheel is made up of a row of eighteenth century stuccoed houses.

Hugging the bridge, The Angel Inn is of the eighteenth century, and the Red Lion Hotel is a fine brick building with a pedimented arch to the riverside street.

Chantry House, behind The Red Lion, was built in 1400 and is timber-framed with an overhanging upper floor.

Victorian boat-houses with gabled and ornamented barge-boards front the river.

Among the many fine buildings throughout the town are the Old Granary in Friday Street, Counters Gardens in Bell Street, Northfield House in Northfield Street and Speaker's House in Hart Street. The Kenton Theatre was built in 1805 and is one of the earliest surviving theatres in the country.

Friday Street Granary, Henley

HENLEY BRIDGE AND THE ANGEL

ROTHERFIELD GREYS

Rotherfield Greys has an Elizabethan manor-house of flint and brick, built by the Knollys family in 1518 on the site of the semi-fortified manor of the De Greys. Part of the original manor remains in the south-west and south-east towers, the keep and part of the north-east tower. There is a maze in the grounds created on the theme of reconciliation by Lady Brunner.

The separated village has a picturesque green and a small church containing the Knollys monument.

ROTHERFIELD PEPPARD

Rotherfield Peppard has a Norman church, rebuilt in 1874. Blount's Court and Crowsley Park are prominent houses.

STOKE ROW

At Stoke Row there is an oriental well presented in 1863 by the Maharajah of Benares, as a gift to E.A. Reade, who had carried out a water scheme in Benares. It has a canopy with an onion dome on eight cast-iron columns, and a cast-iron elephant stands above the drawing machinery.

CHECKENDON

Checkendon is situated high up in the beautiful wooded heart of the Chilterns. The Norman church of St Peter and St Paul is a gem. At one end of the chancel is a Romanesque apse with twelfth-century wall paintings of Christ in Majesty, and the Apostles in procession below. Old flint and brick cottages group around the church.

IPSDEN

Ipsden is a scattered village half-way up the western slopes of the Chilterns. The tiny church of St Mary was built in the late twelfth century, and once belonged to the great Abbey of Bec in Normandy. The Vicarage is of 1700 with five bays of pale red brick. Ipsden House has a circular dovecote of about 1500.

ALL SAINTS CHURCH, ROTHERFIELD PEPPARD

Goring Lock

GORING

Goring is situated where the Thames cuts through a gap in the hills, dividing the Chilterns from the Berkshire Downs. Until the bridge was built about a century ago, there was a ferry here which went back to the times when the Icknield Way crossed the river.

The church of St Thomas of Canterbury is Norman. The Augustinian priory church was demolished at the Dissolution. Other notable buildings include the 1768 Almshouses, a seventeenth-century vicarage, The Miller of Mansfield Hotel and Elvendon Priory.

MAPLEDURHAM

The picturesque village of Mapledurham stands at the end of a winding lane leading down to the banks of the Thames. The cottages and church are dominated by Mapledurham House, a huge Elizabethan mansion begun in 1588 by Sir Michael Blount. It is gabled and of red brick diapered in blue, and has an embattled parapet and many tall chimneys. The sixteenth-century Great Staircase is a feat of construction in oak, built around a square well. On the staircase and first floor are elaborate plastered ceilings of 1612. The manor has been in the same family since 1490. The nearby water-mill is the last working example remaining on the Thames.

WHITCHURCH-ON-THAMES

The village of Whitchurch-on-Thames has a mixture of flint and brick cottages, Georgian houses and Edwardian villas. At the beginning of the twentieth century this part of the Thames became very fashionable, and attracted many new residents.

A cast-iron toll-bridge connects it to Pangbourne in Berkshire. Hardwick Court lies two miles east, and is a handsome Elizabethan gabled house with seventeenth- and eighteenth-century additions.

NORTH STOKE

North Stoke lies on the banks of the Thames looking across to the Downs beyond Moulsford. The church has a beautiful thirteenth-century chancel, and is almost entirely medieval. There are mid-fourteenth-century wall paintings over the chancel arch and, near the pulpit, there is a Martyrdom of St Thomas à Becket. Rectory Farmhouse is of the seventeenth century with an eighteenth-century façade.

SOUTH STOKE

Brunel's railway bridge over the Thames at South Stoke is one of the largest brick bridges ever built.

MAPLEDURHAM HOUSE

EWELME SCHOOL

NUFFIELD

Nuffield is scattered on the hilltop between Nettlebedand Wallingford, and from the churchyard affords splendid panoramic views across the Thames to the Downs. Grims Ditch climbs up through the village. William Morris, the car manufacturer, lived here and took his title as Lord Nuffield from the village.

CROWMARSH GIFFORD

Crowmarsh Gifford stands on the opposite end of the Thames bridge to Wallingford and has a Norman church with several original features remaining. Howbery Court was built in Jacobean style in 1850 with shaped gables, a tower and a cupola.

EWELME

Ewelme lies in a delightful valley just below the Chilterns. At the centre is a magnificent group of buildings comprising the medieval church of St Mary, almshouses and a school. The Duchess of Suffolk, grand-daughter of Geoffrey Chaucer, was responsible for these buildings and is commemorated by a painted and gilded tomb in the church. The tower is the only substantial part of the earlier church remaining.

The Almshouses were built in 1437 to house thirteen poor men, and are arranged around a courtyard, with a timber-framed cloister lining the internal space. The school is a sturdy rectangular two-storey block with diagonal buttresses and tall chimney-stacks. The upper room has a fine arch-braced roof. The Teacher's House includes a stepped gable, and in the garden wall a fifteenth-century moulded brick arch under a battlemented parapet. These buidings all show the influence of Flemish craftsmen, and many parallels can be found in buildings of the same period at Bruges in Belgium.

The manor-house was the home of the Chaucer family, and was used by Henry VIII and Elizabeth I as a country residence. Ford's Farmhouse has a large sixteenth-century weather-boarded barn.

ST MARY'S CHURCH AND ALMSHOUSES, EWELME

BIBLIOGRAPHY

Lethbridge, Richard, *Oxfordshire and Berkshire, Shell Guide*
Mee, Arthur, *Berkshire*
Sherwood, Jennifer, and Pevsner, Nikolaus, *The Buildings of England: Oxfordshire*

THE NUT TREE INN, MURCOTT

INDEX

Numbers in italic indicate illustrations.

THE BEAR, OXFORD